TABLE OF CONTENTS

HOW TO MAKE A QUILT

GETTING STARTED

It seems to me that there are different kinds of baby quilts: heirloom quality, hand quilted, specially designed pieces that probably should be hung on a wall in the nursery and not actually used for the baby, and then the "throw it in the wash every other day until it wears out" kind.

Because of their small size, all of the quilts in this book are pretty quick to complete. Some designs, of course, are faster to make than others. Choose your project based on the intended use of the quilt, whether or not you like the pattern, and on the time available. I make the simpler designs such as *Sunshine and Shadow* and *Building Blocks* to be "used-up," but would prefer that the *Pinwheel Daisy* quilt with its curved seams, appliqué, and hand-quilting become an heirloom. One quilt I gave years ago to a friend's baby was never used by that child, but subsequently became the beloved "bankie" of his little sister, a child I didn't meet until she was 7 years old. By then the quilt was in shreds, but there was magic in knowing my quilt was that important in the life of a child.

Each quilt pattern, beginning on page 12, gives instructions for one size of quilt. There are square "receiving" quilts for infants and longer rectangular quilts appropriate for napping children up to age five or six. Change the size of the projects by adding or subtracting rows of blocks, or by changing the number and width of the borders.

Color and Fabric

You may want to make a quilt exactly the way it looks in the book; in that case, just follow the materials list provided with the pattern. For the most part, I have used 1930s reproduction prints to create a light and pretty look. To get a variety of pastel colors and prints, I collected fat quarters and variety packs from several quilt stores. Many of these prints, called "conversationals," are covered with fun little animals, children and storybook characters.

If you are like many quilters, though, you may want to use different colors and prints than those described in the quilt patterns. To choose your own fabrics and colors, study the quilt pattern instructions. The materials list will tell how many different colors or value groups are needed. The pattern may call for assorted dark blues, for instance, but you could substitute assorted dark reds instead. If so, gather as many red prints in differing intensities and visual textures as possible. Not every piece will be used, but it is important to study the possibilities. Do the same with each color or value group in the quilt design.

The quilts in this book are made of lightweight, closely woven, 100% cotton fabrics. Preshrink and color test your fabric before you use it. Wash lights and darks separately with mild detergent and warm water. If you suspect the dark colors might run, rinse those fabrics repeatedly in clear water until the dye-loss stops. Dry fabrics in the dryer and press them well before cutting.

What is a Fat Quarter Yard?

Divide a yard of fabric (36" x 44") in half the long way; then divide each resulting section in half to make 4 fat quarters, each measuring 18" x 22". Quilters like fat quarters because they provide more useable fabric than quarter yards measured off the bolt at 9". Quilting stores sell precut fat quarters one at a time or in coordinated packets.

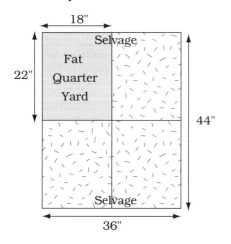

ROTARY CUTTING

Most of the pieced patterns in this book were chosen and sized with no-template rotary cutting in mind. Templates for the patches have been provided mainly for checking purposes, though they are certainly suitable for template-based techniques as well.

It helps to cut at a table that you can walk around to easily position yourself for safe and efficient cutting. Think also about your posture and table height as you cut. Stand (you'll have more control than when sitting) comfortably with your head and body centered at the cutting line. Many quilters find they are more comfortable and can work longer if the cutting table is higher than a normal sewing table. You will need to experiment to find the table height that is best for you.

When making all cuts, fabric should be placed to your right and the ruler to the left. (If you are left handed, reverse the directions.) Hold ruler down firmly with left hand. Move your left hand along the ruler as you make the cut, applying pressure near where you are cutting to keep the ruler from slipping. Keep your fingers clear of the cutting edge and keep the ruler accurately positioned on the fabric. Use a firm, even pressure as you cut. Begin rolling the cutter before you reach the fabric edge and continue across. Remember to roll the cutter away from you. The blade is very sharp, so be careful!

Safety First!

1. *Keep the safety shield on the rotary cutter when it is not in use.*
2. *Roll the cutter away from yourself. Plan your cutting so your fingers, hands, arms or other body parts are never at risk.*
3. *Keep the cutter out of the reach of children.*
4. *Dispose of used blades in a responsible manner. Wrap and tape cardboard around them before putting them in the garbage, or better yet, recycle. Resharpening services are advertised in various quilt magazines.*

Straight Grain and Bias

Fabric is made of threads (the technical term is yarns) woven together. Threads that run the length of the fabric, parallel to the selvage, are lengthwise straight grain. Those that run across the fabric are crosswise straight grain. All other grains are considered bias. True bias runs at a 45° angle to the two straight grains. For the small pieces in patchwork, both kinds of straight grain are considered equal. For long strips for borders and lattices, however, it is best to use the lengthwise grain as it is the more stable (less stretchy) of the two.

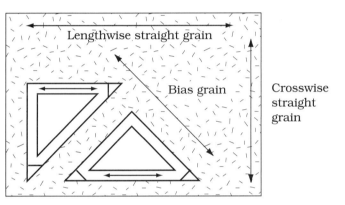

Bias stretches and straight grain holds its shape, so fabric pieces should be cut with one or more edges aligned with the straight grain of the fabric. The straight grain should fall on the outside edge of any pieced unit. This applies to pieced units, design blocks, set pieces in the larger quilt, and the edge pieces in pieced borders. Templates in this book are marked with grain line arrows.

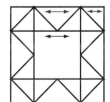 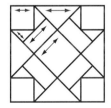

Cutting Straight Strips

The rotary method of cutting squares and rectangles begins with cutting strips of fabric. In quilt construction, long strips of fabric are used for borders, and shorter ones are used for lattices. Narrow strips are used in some design blocks. Strips can be cut on the lengthwise grain (parallel to the selvage) or crosswise grain (perpendicular to the selvage). All strips are cut with the 1/4" seam allowance included.

To cut strips on lengthwise grain, fold the fabric so cuts will be parallel to the selvage. Trim away selvage and make successive cuts measuring from the first cut.

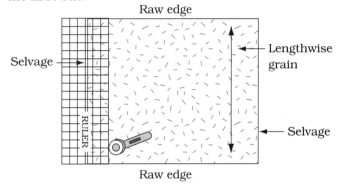

Squares and Rectangles

First cut fabric in strips the finished measurement of the square plus seam allowances. Using the square plastic cutting ruler, cut fabric into squares the same width of the strip. Cut rectangles in the same manner, first cutting strips the length of the rectangle plus seam allowances, then cutting to the proper width.

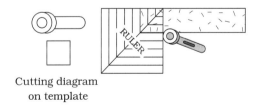

Cutting diagram
on template

Note: *Templates are given with the quilt patterns. Those that are easily rotary cut display a cutting diagram of a rotary cutter, a picture of how the shape is cut and cutting dimensions.*

Triangles

Half-Square Triangles

If you need a triangle with the straight grain on the short side, cut half-square triangles. Cut a square the measurement given in the pattern and then cut it in half diagonally. The resulting two triangles will have short sides on the straight grain of the fabric and the long side on the bias. Check the first triangles cut against the templates provided to make sure they are the right size.

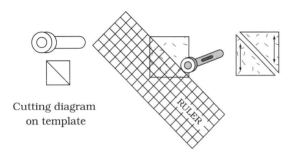

Cutting diagram
on template

Quarter-Square Triangles

If you need a triangle with the straight grain on the long side, cut quarter-square triangles. Cut a square the measurement given in the pattern, then cut it diagonally, corner to corner. Without moving the resulting triangles, line up the ruler and make another diagonal cut in the opposite direction. The resulting four triangles will have the long side on the straight grain and the short sides on the bias.

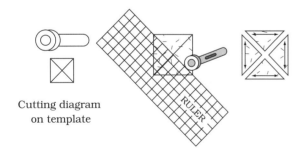

Cutting diagram
on template

Trimming Points for Easy Matching

Though I trim points on triangles to take the guesswork out of matching patches before stitching, points have been left on the shapes to aid with measuring for rotary cutting. The templates with the quilt patterns all have appropriate trim points indicated. Use a template or ruler to trim 3/8" points off these triangles for easy matching as shown below.

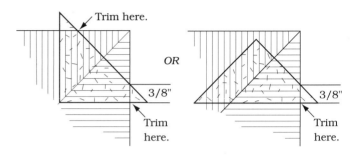

MACHINE PIECING

General Rules for Sewing

1. Use 100% cotton white or neutral-colored thread as light as the lightest fabric in the project. Use dark neutral thread for piecing dark solids. I choose one color of thread and use it to piece the whole quilt regardless of color changes in the fabric. Lighter threads, if they don't get trimmed completely, will not show through light fabrics in the finished quilt.
2. Clip threads as you sew. Make it a habit. Threads left hanging from the ends of seam lines can get in the way and be a real nuisance.

Accuracy Test

To test your seam allowance, cut three 1-1/2" squares. Sew them together with your best 1/4" seam allowance. Press the seams and measure the resulting strip: it should be 3-1/2" long. If it isn't, try it again with a deeper or shallower seam.

3-1/2"

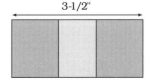

3. Sew 1/4" seams. To establish the proper seam allowance on your sewing machine, place a paper template with the proper 1/4" seam allowance or a piece of quarter- or eighth-inch graph paper under the presser foot and gently lower the needle onto the seam line. The distance from the needle to the edge of the paper is 1/4". Lay a piece of masking tape at the edge of the paper to act as the 1/4" guide. I use a scant (by two threads or so) 1/4" seam allowance for the most accurate results.

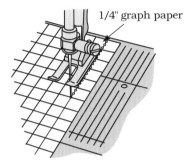

1/4" graph paper

4. For most piecing, sew from cut edge to cut edge. Backtack if you wish, but when a seam line will be crossed and held by another, it is not necessary.

5. Use chain piecing whenever possible to save time and thread. To chain piece, sew one seam, but do not lift the presser foot. Do not take the piece out of the sewing machine and do not cut the thread. Instead, set up the next seam to be sewn and stitch as you did the first. There will be a little twist of thread between the two pieces. Sew all the seams you can at one time in this way, then remove the "chain." Clip the threads.

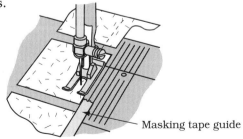

Masking tape guide

6. To piece a unit block, sew the smallest pieces together first to form units. Join smaller units to form larger ones until the block is complete. (See piecing diagrams with each design block in quilt patterns.)

Beginning and Ending Scraps

When you are piecing, stitch over a folded scrap of fabric before the first seam and after the last. End stitching in the middle of the second scrap. Leave it in the machine, snip the sewn patches free: the ending scrap is now the beginning scrap for your next seam. This little trick helps your machine start stitching at the edge of the fabric, saves thread and helps keep your sewing area thread free!

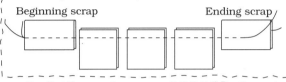

Beginning scrap   Ending scrap

Pinning

In general pin seams before stitching when matching is involved, if your seams are longer than 4", or if you are at all unsure. Pin points of matching (where seam lines or points meet) first. Once these important points are firmly in place, pin the rest of the seam, easing if necessary. Keep pins away from seam lines, as sewing over them tends to damage the needle and makes it hard to be accurate in tight places.

Pressing

In general press seams to one side, toward the darker fabric whenever possible. It is easier to press to one side, it puts the seam-line stress on fabric instead of stitches, and prevents a shadow line of the darker fabric from showing through the lighter.

The two main exceptions to the general rule of pressing to the dark are when seams are pressed open to distribute bulk, as in the feather rows of Feathered Stars or the center seam of a Pinwheel, and when, for matching purposes, seams are pressed in opposite directions, regardless of which is the darker fabric.

For patchwork, I press with a dry iron that has a shot of steam when needed. Take care not to overpress. Over-enthusiastic pressing can stretch and distort fabric pieces, as well as make the fabric shiny where there are bumps.

Matching

The following matching techniques can be helpful in many different piecing situations:

1. **Opposing Seams.** When seam lines need to match, press seam allowances in opposite directions before stitching. The two "opposing" seams will hold each other in place and evenly distribute the bulk.

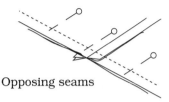

Opposing seams

2. **Positioning Pin.** A pin, carefully pushed straight and pulled right through two points that need to match, will establish the proper point of matching. Pin the seam normally and remove the positioning pin before stitching.

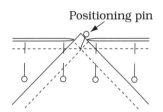

Positioning pin

3. **The X.** When triangles are pieced, stitches will form an X at the next seam line. Stitch through the center of the X to make sure the points on the sewn triangles will not be chopped off. When seams are pressed to one side, the X will look like it does below. Sew right through the point indicated for crisply pieced points. Sew with these seams on top so the X can be seen clearly.

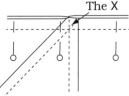

The X

4. **Easing.** When two pieces to be sewn together are supposed to match but instead are slightly different lengths, pin the points of matching and stitch with the shorter piece on top. The feed dog eases the fullness of the bottom piece.

Piecing Pinwheels

Here's a little trick for making the eight triangle points in the center of the Pinwheel block come together accurately.

1. With the bias-strip piecing method, make 4 two-triangle squares.

2. Matching diagonal, opposing seams, chain piece 2 halves of the pinwheel. Make sure the triangles meet exactly at the 1/4" seam line.

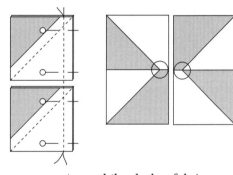

3. Press seams toward the darker fabric.

4. With right sides together, use a positioning pin to match the points of the triangles at the center seams. Opposing vertical and diagonal seams will "nest." Pin as shown. Stitch center seam through the X. Press center seam open.

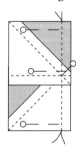
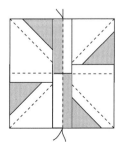

Bias-Strip Piecing Method

The instructions for four designs (Stars and Pinwheels, School House and the two Sailboats) in this book are written using the bias-strip piecing method to make two-triangle square units. This is a nifty technique I have used for many years to make these pieced squares quickly and accurately. You may prefer to cut triangles and sew them together for the squares you need, but believe me, once you get used to this method, you'll never want to cut triangles again!

Use these instructions to make the two-triangle squares for the Stars and Pinwheels Quilt (page 12), the School House Quilt (page 31) and the Sailboat Wall Quilt (page 44). Bias strip piecing is also used in the Sailboat Quilt (page 40), but the cutting dimensions and the number of strips are different, so follow the directions with the pattern and refer to this page for general technique.

1. Place two 7" squares (1 background and 1 print) right sides together. Both layers will be cut at the same time.
2. With a rotary cutter and ruler, cut the squares diagonally, corner to corner. Measuring from the center diagonal cut, cut strips 2" wide as shown.

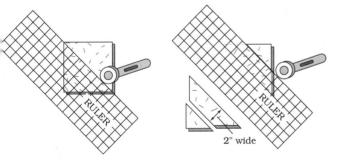

2" wide

3. Pick up pairs of contrasting strips; they will be right sides together and ready to stitch. Sew them together on the long bias edge, using 1/4" seam allowance. Stitch corner triangles together. Press seams toward the darker fabric. Sew bias strip pairs together as shown and press.

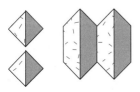

4. Using a square cutting ruler and rotary cutter, cut 8 two-triangle units 2" square from the sewn strips. Place the ruler's diagonal line over the seam line. Cut squares slightly (a few threads to 1/8") larger than the desired cut size of the two-triangle square unit. Make two cuts to separate the square from the sewn strips. (Let your rotary cutter go a few threads beyond the seam line on each cut to cleanly separate the square without leaving a maddening two threads uncut.)

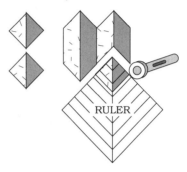

RULER

5. Turn each square so the two sides you just cut are toward you. Align the diagonal line of the square rotary cutting ruler with the seam line of the square and the exact dimension (2") on the ruler with the cut sides of the square. Make the final two cuts.

RULER

6. Repeat until 7 squares have been cut (5 squares will come from the strips and 2 squares will come from the triangles that were sewn together). You will have 2 triangles leftover from the sides of the strips. Join them on the long sides and cut another square.

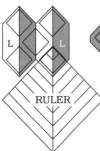

RULER

Stitch leftover edge triangles together to make 8th square.

COMPLETING THE QUILT TOP

Setting the Quilt Together

When sewn quilt blocks are joined together to make a quilt top, it is called the "set." One way to set the design blocks is to sew them together side by side. In other sets, design blocks can be separated by set pieces, which can be unpieced squares, rectangles or triangles. Sets can be straight or diagonal. Alternate blocks the same size as the design blocks can be placed between them in checkerboard fashion. Diagonal sets using alternate blocks require side triangles to complete the set. Strips of fabric, called lattices, can also be used to separate the unit blocks. Set pieces can be pieced in different ways to add to the overall design.

Whatever set you choose for your quilt, the general construction rules for sewing blocks still apply.

1. Sew exact 1/4" seams edge to edge.
2. Look for the longest seams to establish piecing units.
3. Keep straight grain on the outside edges of the quilt sections.
4. Press for opposing seams.
5. Pin all points of matching.

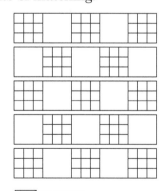

Blocks set in straight rows

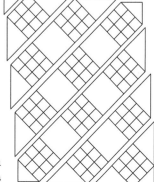

Blocks set in diagonal rows

Borders

Cut border strips from the lengthwise grain of the fabric. Cut them longer than you think you'll need and trim to fit later.

For plain borders with straight-sewn corners, first sew borders to the long sides of the quilt, then to the top and bottom. To find the proper length of borders with blunt-sewn corners, first measure the length of the quilt through the center, edge to edge (including seam allowances). Cut both side strips this length and stitch them to the sides of the quilt. To measure for the top and bottom, take the dimension across the center of the quilt (including the side borders and seam allowances). Cut the borders this length and stitch. It is not uncommon to have to ease one side of a quilt to fit a border and stretch the opposite side slightly to fit the same dimension.

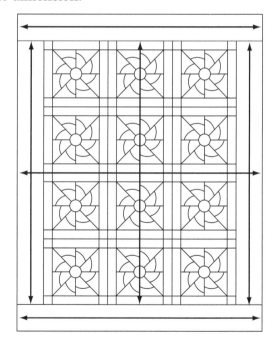

When pinning borders in place for sewing, I like to work at the ironing board. Pin the quilt to the board to keep it from slipping. Position the border on the quilt by matching centers, ends, and important points of matching. Ease and generously pin everything in between. Pressing the border to the quilt top with a steam iron at this point helps the two fit together and makes the sewing go more smoothly. Steam both shrinks and stretches fabric, allowing you to adjust the fit where it is needed.

LAYERING THE QUILT

Batting

Batting is the filler between the quilt top and the backing. It is commonly made of cotton or polyester or a combination of the two. Check at your local quilt or fabric store for batting and read the labels for fiber content, size, thickness, how close quilting must be and special handling instructions. Thick or high-loft batting is used in comforters that are tied. Thin or low-loft batting is used in quilts that are quilted by hand or machine.

The cotton-polyester combination batting is said to combine the best features of the two fibers. Cotton or cotton-poly batts are the fiber of choice for machine quilting because they don't slip around like polyester.

Backing

You can use a single length of 45"-wide fabric for backing small quilts. To be safe, plan on a usable width of only 40" to 42" after shrinkage. Choose light fabrics to back quilts with a lot of white in them. Very dark backings can show through batting to the quilt top and it just doesn't look good. Also keep in mind that your quilting will really show up if you use plain fabrics on the back of the quilt. If your quilting is less than perfect and you don't want to showcase it this way, choose a busy print for the backing as camouflage.

Layering and Basting

After marking the quilt top for quilting (see Quilting page 10), baste the three layers of the quilt together. Lay the backing face down on a large, clean, flat surface — the floor or a large table. With masking tape, tape the backing down to keep it smooth and flat while you are working with the other layers. Gently lay the batting on top of the backing, centering and smoothing it as you go. It is a good idea to let the batt "relax" for a few hours at this point, to ease out wrinkles. Trim batting to size of backing.

Center the freshly ironed quilt top on top of the batting, right side up. Starting in the middle, use straight pins to secure the three layers together while gently smoothing out fullness to the sides

and corners. Take care not to distort the straight lines of the quilt design and the borders.

After pinning, baste the layers together with needle and light-colored thread. Start in the middle and make a line of long stitches to each corner to form a large X. Continue basting in a grid of parallel lines 6" apart. Finish with a row of basting around the outside edges —1/4" away from the edge. Quilts that are to be quilted with a hoop or on your lap will be handled more than those quilted on a frame, and they will require more basting. After basting, remove the pins. Now you are ready to quilt.

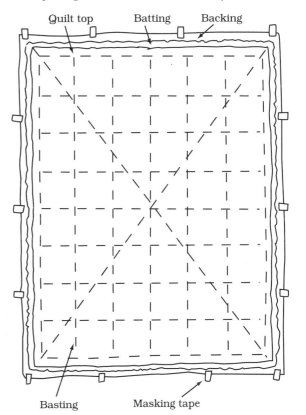

Quilt top   Batting   Backing

Basting   Masking tape

QUILTING

Quilting is the process of stitching the three layers of the quilt together. Each line of quilting stitches creates a shadow depression in the quilt surface. Quilted areas recede; unquilted areas stand out or come forward.

Where you place the quilting lines will depend on the patchwork design, the type of batting used, and how much quilting you want to do. Quilting lines should be evenly distributed over the quilt surface. Directions that come with your batting will tell how close the quilting lines must be to keep the batt from coming apart when the quilt is washed. The styles of quilting that I use in my quilts are: outline quilting (in the ditch or 1/4" away from every seam), allover designs and an occasional quilting motif to fit a specific space.

Mark your quilt top before it is assembled with the backing and batting. You will need marking pencils; a long ruler or yardstick; stencils or templates for quilting motifs; and a smooth, clean, hard surface on which to work. Thoroughly press the quilt top. Use a sharp marking pencil and lightly mark the quilting lines on the fabric. No matter what kind of marking tool you use, light lines will be easier to remove than heavy ones.

Outline quilting doesn't have to be marked, though many quilters use 1/4"-wide masking tape to help keep their lines straight. Straight lines are easy to mark with long straight rulers. Curved-line motifs such as the Pumpkin Seed and the Clamshell require stencils or templates.

Hand Quilting

To quilt by hand, you will need quilting thread, quilting needles, small scissors, a thimble, and perhaps a balloon or large rubber band to help grasp the needle if it gets stuck. Quilt on a frame or a large hoop. I generally quilt long lines on a big frame, but if I have small multi-directional quilting motifs, I quilt them on a hoop after the quilt is removed from the larger frame.

Use a single strand of quilting thread not longer than 18". Make a small single knot in the end of the thread. To begin, insert the needle in the top layer about 3/4" from the point you want to start stitching. Pull the needle out at the starting point

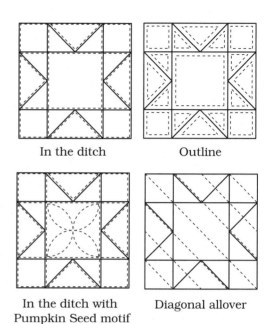

In the ditch   Outline

In the ditch with   Diagonal allover
Pumpkin Seed motif

and gently tug at the knot until it pops through the fabric and is buried in the batting. Make a backstitch and begin quilting. The quilting stitch is a small running stitch that goes through all three layers of the quilt. Take two, three, or even four stitches at a time if you can keep them even. When crossing seams, you might find it necessary to "hunt and peck" one stitch at a time. Stitches should be small (8-10 per inch is good), even, and straight. Concentrate on making even and straight stitches; tiny stitches will come with practice.

When you come almost to the end of the thread, make a single knot 1/4" from the fabric. Take a backstitch to bury the knot in the batting. Run the thread through the batting and out the quilt top; snip it off. The first and last stitches will look different from the running stitches in between. To make them less noticeable, start and stop where quilting lines cross each other or at seam joints.

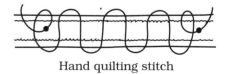

Hand quilting stitch

Machine Quilting

Machine quilting is perfect for small baby quilts that need to be durable. Plan a simple quilting design that involves continuous long straight lines, gentle curves and few direction changes.

Choose 100% cotton or 80% cotton/20% polyester batting. Baste your quilt thoroughly as described on page 9.

Use 100% cotton threads in colors that will blend with fabrics in the quilt. This might mean choosing several colors of thread and changing for each section of quilting. DMC 50 Embroidery thread gives a smooth look to the work.

Read the machine's instruction manual for special tension settings for sewing through thicknesses. Put a fresh needle in before you begin and use an *even feed* or *walking foot* attachment to evenly feed the layers. If your machine has this feature, set it to stop with the needle down.

Working on a large table that will support the weight of the quilt, stitch all the long lines first. Outline borders, blocks and lattices "in the ditch" to secure them over the entire quilt before you begin working on smaller areas. Periodically take the quilt to the ironing board for pressing.

BINDING

After quilting, use a rotary cutter and a long ruler to trim excess batting and backing even with the edge of the quilt top.

Making the Binding

The fabric binding used to finish the edges of a quilt is usually made from bias strips. To find the true bias use a ruler with a 45°-angle marking. Using a rotary cutter and mat, cut 1-1/2"-wide strips along the bias. One-half yard of fabric will yield 5-1/4 yards of 1-1/2"-wide bias binding. Seam ends together to make a continuous strip long enough to go around your quilt, with a few extra inches for joining.

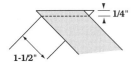

Binding the Quilt Edges

1. Using a 1/4" seam allowance, sew the binding strips to the front of the quilt. An *even feed* or *walking foot* on your machine will help feed the quilt layers evenly without pleating. Begin at the center of one side and sew through all layers. Be careful not to stretch the bias or the quilt edge as you sew. Begin stitching about 2" from the end of the bias binding strip and stitch until you reach the 1/4" seam allowance point at the corner. Backstitch; cut threads.

2. Turn quilt. Fold the binding away from the quilt, then fold again to place binding along edge of quilt. (This fold creates an angled pleat at the corner.)

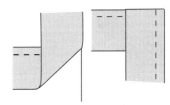

3. Stitch from the edge of the quilt along the seam line to the 1/4" seam allowance point at the next corner. Backstitch; cut threads. Fold binding as in step 2 and continue around edge up to 3" before the starting point. Backtack.

4. Join the beginning and ending of the binding strip, either with a machine or hand sewn seam. Or overlap one end over the other.

5. Turn binding to the back side, turning raw edge under, and blindstitch in place. At each corner, fold binding as shown to form a miter on back of quilt.

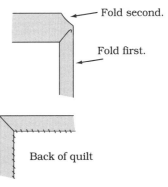

Fold second.

Fold first.

Back of quilt

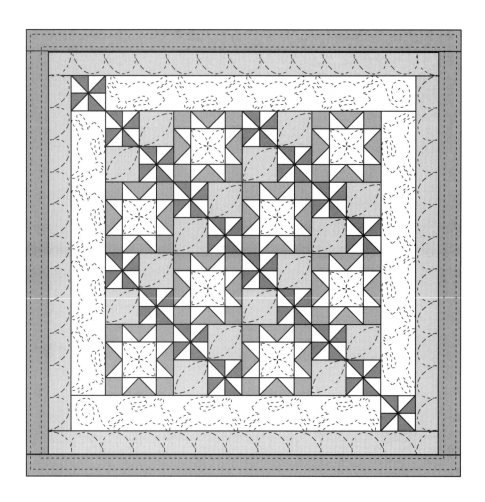

Stars and Pinwheels Quilt

I think square baby quilts are better than rectangular quilts for swaddling infants. If you want to make this quilt rectangular or larger for an older child, just add more rows of blocks.

I chose blue, white and yellow for the quilt pictured on page 29. It is cheerful and soft with a bit of a twinkle. Two different yellows prints, four blues and one white will do the trick.

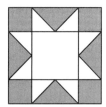

Evening Star
6" block
Make 8.

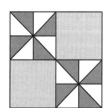

Double Pinwheel
6" block
Make 8.

Pinwheel
3" block
Make 2.

DIMENSIONS: 38" x 38"

MATERIALS: 42"-wide 100% cotton, color tested and preshrunk

Yellow print #1 for Evening Star blocks: fat quarter yard
Yellow print #2 for inner border: 1/2 yard
Blue print #1 for Evening Star block backgrounds: fat quarter yard
Blue print #2 for large squares in Double Pinwheel blocks and middle border: 3/4 yard
Blue print #3 for Pinwheels: 1/2 yard
Blue print #4 for outer border: 1/2 yard
White print for Pinwheels: 1/2 yard
Backing: 1-1/4 yards
Binding: 1/2 yard to make 160 inches of 1-1/2"-wide bias binding
Batting: 42" x 42"
Thread for piecing and quilting

DIRECTIONS

BLOCKS
Cutting amounts for one block are given first.
Amounts for whole quilt are listed in parentheses.

Evening Star: Make eight 6" Evening Star blocks.

From yellow print #1, cut:
1 (8) square(s), 3-1/2" x 3-1/2" (Template #1)
4 (32) squares, 2-3/8" x 2-3/8", cut diagonally to
   yield 8 (64) half-square triangles (Template #2)

From blue print #1, cut:
4 (32) squares, 2" x 2" (Template #3)
1 (8) square(s), 4-1/4" x 4-1/4", cut diagonally
   twice to make 4 (32) quarter-square triangles
   (Template #4)

Piecing the Evening Stars:
1. With yellow #2 triangles and blue #4 triangles,
   make 32 three-triangle units. Press seams away
   from large triangle.

2. Arrange pieced triangle units with yellow #1
   squares and blue #3 squares in star design.
   Join pieces in rows as shown. Join the rows
   together.

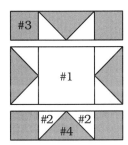

Double Pinwheel: Make eight 6" Double Pinwheel
blocks and two 3" Pinwheel blocks.

From blue print #2, cut:
2 (16) squares, 3-1/2" x 3-1/2" (Template #1)

From blue print #3, cut:
1 (9) square(s), 7" x 7", for bias-strip piecing
   two-triangle square units (Template #3)

From white print, cut:
1 (9) square(s), 7" x 7", for bias-strip piecing
   two-triangle square units (Template #3)

Piecing the Pinwheels:
1. Follow the directions on page 7 for bias-strip
   piecing to make 72 two-triangle square units
   that measure 2" x 2" (Template #3). Repeat
   steps 1 through 6 nine times.

Note: *If you prefer not to do bias-strip piecing, use
Template #2 to cut 72 triangles from blue print
#3 and 72 triangles from the white print. Join
white and blue triangles to make two-triangle
squares.*

2. Using the 72 two-triangle squares, make
   eighteen 3" Pinwheel units as shown on page 6.
   Set 2 units aside for inner border.

3. Arrange pieced Pinwheels and blue #1 squares
   in Double Pinwheel design. Join Pinwheels to
   squares as shown, then join halves together
   with a center seam.

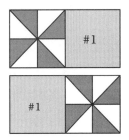

QUILT ASSEMBLY

Arrange the finished blocks in rows as shown in the Quilt Assembly Diagram, alternating Evening Star and Double Pinwheel blocks. Sew the rows together to finish the center section of the quilt.

BORDERS

Inner Border: From yellow print #2, cut two strips 3-1/2" x 24-1/2" for the side borders and two strips 3-1/2" x 27-1/2" for the top and bottom. (Measure your quilt before cutting! See Borders, page 8.) Join border strips to sides of quilt first. To each top and bottom strip, join a Pinwheel block. Stitch to top and bottom of quilt center as shown.

Middle Border: From blue print #2, cut two strips 2-1/2" x 30-1/2" for the side borders and two strips 2-1/2" x 34-1/2" for the top and bottom. Join border strips to sides of quilt first, then to top and bottom.

Outer Border: From blue print #3, cut two strips 2-1/2" x 34-1/2" for the side borders and two strips 2-1/2" x 38-1/2" for the top and bottom. Join border strips to sides of quilt first, then to top and bottom.

FINISHING

1. Plan and mark quilting design. The quilt shown in color on page 29 was mostly outline quilted. The Evening Star center square contains a Pumpkin Seed motif. The large squares in the Double Pinwheel blocks contain large leaf shapes. The inner borders sport 6"-long bunnies and the middle border has a Bunny Hop design.
2. Layer batting, backing and quilt top. Baste.
3. Quilt by hand or machine.
4. Cut 160 inches of 1-1/2"-wide bias strips for binding. Bind quilt edge.

Quilt Assembly Diagram

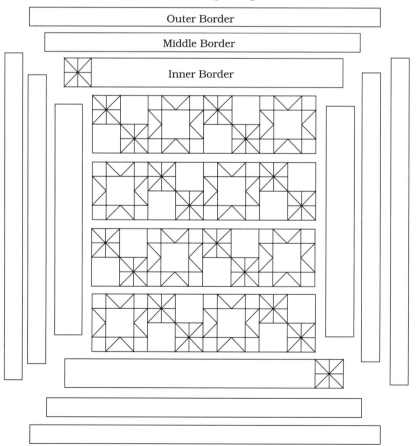

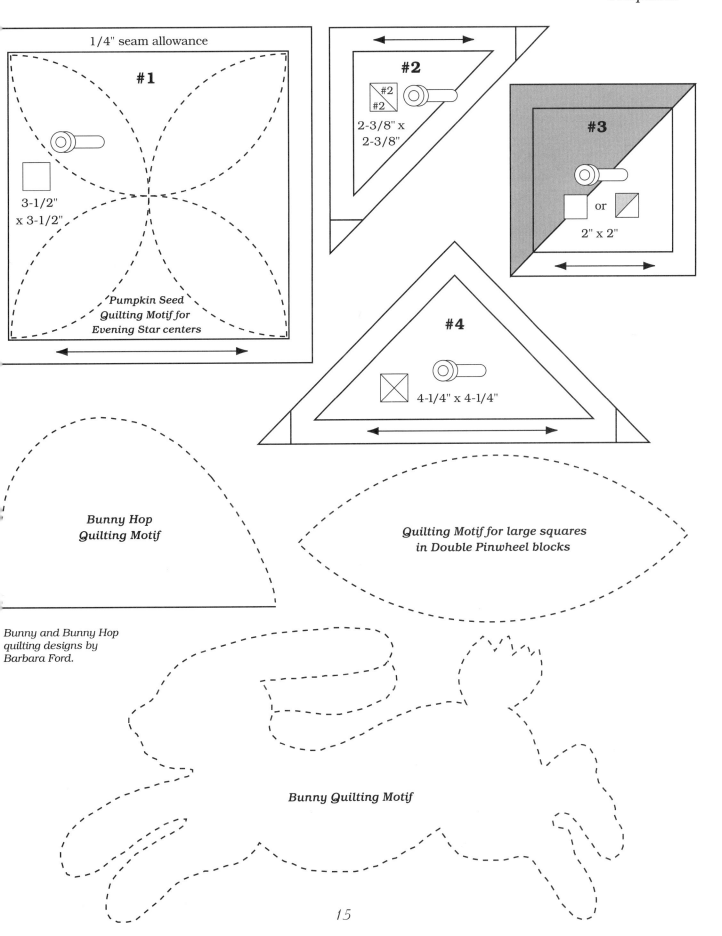

1/4" seam allowance

#1

3-1/2" x 3-1/2"

Pumpkin Seed Quilting Motif for Evening Star centers

#2

#2 #2

2-3/8" x 2-3/8"

#3

or

2" x 2"

#4

4-1/4" x 4-1/4"

Bunny Hop Quilting Motif

Quilting Motif for large squares in Double Pinwheel blocks

Bunny and Bunny Hop quilting designs by Barbara Ford.

Bunny Quilting Motif

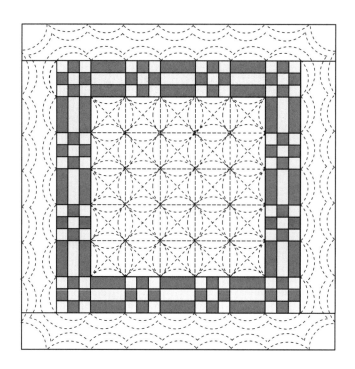

Building Blocks Quilt

If you've never made a quilt before or just want an easy project, this little quilt is a wonderful place to start. The design pairs Ninepatch and Rail Fence blocks in a border that is perfect for strip piecing. (If you prefer not to strip piece these blocks, you'll find templates on page 19.) The large plain center square is a good place to showcase a special print, picture panel or lots of machine quilting. Then choose a pretty flannel for the backing and you've got a great baby gift!

DIMENSIONS: 40" x 40"

MATERIALS: 42"-wide 100% cotton, color tested and preshrunk

Blue print for blocks: 1/2 yard
White for blocks: 1/2 yard
Pink stripe for center and borders: 1-1/2 yards
Backing: 1-1/4 yards
Binding: 1/2 yard blue plaid to make 170 inches of 1-1/2"-wide bias binding
Batting: 44" x 44"
Thread for piecing and quilting

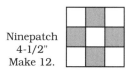

Ninepatch
4-1/2"
Make 12.

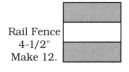

Rail Fence
4-1/2"
Make 12.

DIRECTIONS

BLOCKS

Ninepatch and Rail Fence: Make 12 Ninepatch blocks and 12 Rail Fence blocks. Though the shapes in the blocks could easily be cut individually, it is easy to strip piece the units. The following cutting instructions are for the whole quilt:

From blue print, cut:
13 strips, each 2" wide, from the lengthwise grain of the fabric (approximately 18" long).

From white, cut:
11 strips, each 2" wide, from the lengthwise grain of the fabric.

From pink stripe, cut:
1 square, 23" x 23"
4 border strips, each 4-3/4" wide, from the lengthwise grain of the fabric. (If the useable width of your fabric is not 42", you will have to choose a slightly narrower width for the border strips.)

Piecing the blocks:

1. Using the 2"-wide strips, make 5 strip sets that are blue-white-blue (A) and 3 strip sets that are white-blue-white (B). Join strips together on the long sides using a 1/4" seam allowance.

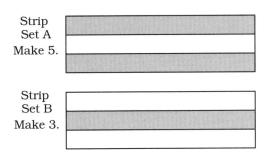

Strip Set A Make 5.

Strip Set B Make 3.

2. To make 12 Rail Fence blocks, cut three 5" sections from each of 4 Strip Sets A. Save remaining length for Ninepatch blocks.

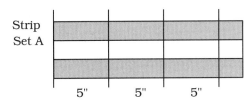

Strip Set A

5"　5"　5"

3. To make 12 Ninepatch blocks:

   • Cut twelve 2" sections from the remaining portions of Strip Sets A.

   • Cut twenty-four 2" sections from Strip Sets B.

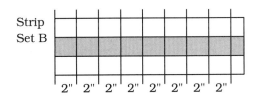

Strip Set B

2" 2" 2" 2" 2" 2" 2" 2"

   • For each Ninepatch block, join two 2" sections from Strip Set B with one 2" section from Strip Set A as shown. Repeat 12 times.

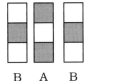

B　A　B　　Make 12.

QUILT ASSEMBLY

1. Arrange the 24 finished blocks around the center square as shown in the Quilt Assembly Diagram. Alternate Rail Fence and Ninepatch blocks in rows. Join the side rows of blocks (5 blocks each) to the center first, then sew the top and bottom rows (7 blocks each).

2. Measure and trim two 4-3/4"-wide outer border strips for the sides. Join to quilt center. Then measure and trim remaining 4-3/4"-wide outer border strips and add them to the center. (See Borders, page 8.)

Quilt Assembly Diagram

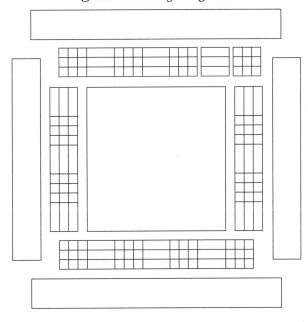

FINISHING

1. Plan and mark quilting design. Use outline quilting for the pieced borders. In the center square, mark a grid of 4-1/2" squares. Draw diagonal lines through all the squares. Make a stiffened template of the Template for Quilting Design on page 19 to mark curved lines in the center squares and border.

2. Layer batting, backing and quilt top. Baste.

3. Quilt by hand or machine.

4. Cut 170 inches of 1-1/2"-wide bias strips for binding.

5. Bind quilt edge.

Ninepatch Doll Quilt

The leftover scraps from the Building Blocks Quilt will probably be enough to make this easy little doll quilt. Gently curved lines in the quilting make it a great project on which to practice machine piecing skills.

DIMENSIONS: 17" x 17"

MATERIALS: 42"-wide 100% cotton, color tested and preshrunk
Blue print for blocks: 1/8 yard
White for blocks and setting pieces:
    fat quarter yard
Pink print for inner borders: 4 strips, 1" x 15"
    (length will be trimmed to fit)
Pink stripe for outer borders: 4 strips, 2" x 18"
    (length will be trimmed to fit)
Backing: fat quarter yard
Binding: fat quarter yard blue plaid to make
    78 inches of 1-1/2"-wide bias binding
Batting: 20" x 20"
Thread for piecing and quilting

DIRECTIONS

BLOCKS

Make 4 Ninepatch blocks. Use any leftover pieced units from the Building Blocks quilt or cut all new pieces from the leftover fabric. Cutting instructions are for the whole quilt.

From blue print, cut:
20 squares, 2" x 2" (Template #1)

From white, cut:
16 squares, 2" x 2" (Template #1)
1 square, 5" x 5" (Template #3)
1 square, 7-5/8" x 7-5/8", cut twice diagonally to
    yield 4 quarter-square triangles (Template #4)
2 squares, 4" x 4", cut once diagonally to yield 4
    half-square triangles (Template #5)

Piecing the blocks:
1. Using the blue and white 2" squares, piece
   4 Ninepatch blocks as shown.

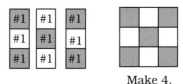

Make 4.

QUILT ASSEMBLY & FINISHING

1. Arrange the blocks and setting pieces (#3, #4 and #5) in diagonal rows, and join rows as shown in the Quilt Assembly Diagram below.
2. Measure and trim to fit 1"-wide pink print border strips. Join to quilt center. Then measure and trim white 2"-wide strips for the outer borders and add them to the center. (See Borders, page 8)
3. Plan and mark quilting design. Layer batting, backing and quilt top. Baste. Quilt by hand or machine. Cut 78 inches of 1-1/2"-wide bias strips for binding. Bind quilt edge.

Quilt Assembly Diagram

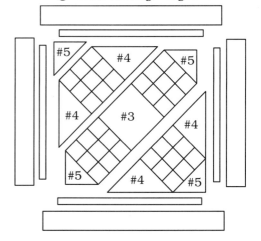

Templates

Note: *If you prefer to use templates rather than strip piecing for the Building Blocks Quilt on page 16, use Templates #1 and #2 for the Ninepatch and Rail Fence blocks.*

1/4" seam allowance

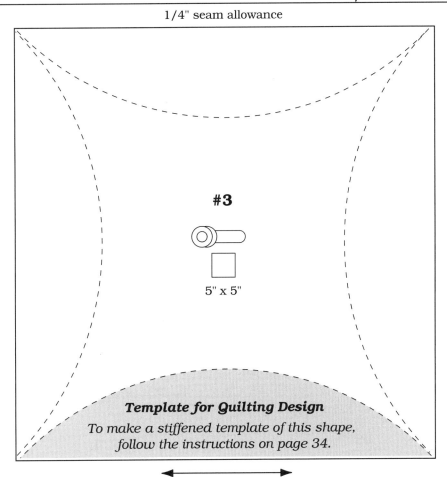

#3

5" x 5"

Template for Quilting Design
To make a stiffened template of this shape, follow the instructions on page 34.

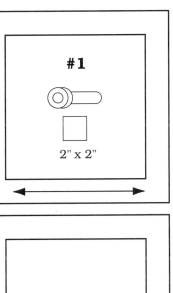

#1

2" x 2"

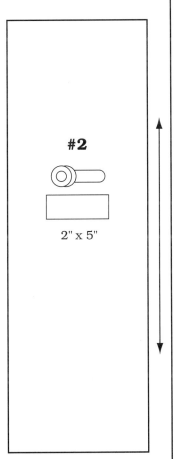

#2

2" x 5"

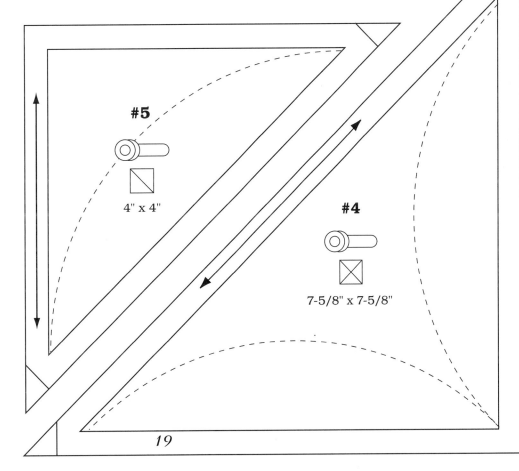

#5

4" x 4"

#4

7-5/8" x 7-5/8"

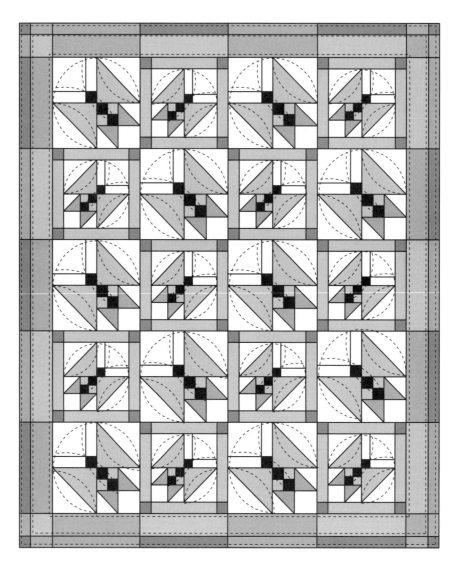

Katie's Butterfly Quilt

Butterfly patterns were popular in the 1930s and 1940s. Often they were appliquéd and edged with a buttonhole stitch in black embroidery thread. My pieced Butterfly pattern is the one I made for my granddaughter, Katie Rose, before she was born. The quilt design includes two alternating Butterfly blocks made of scrappy 1930s reproduction prints. While shopping for the fabrics, I bought fat quarters or fat eighths to get the variety I wanted. I tried to get a large-scale print, a small scale print and a plaid or a stripe in each color group. Traditional unbleached muslin was used for the block backgrounds and a solid black for the three squares that are the Butterfly's "body."

DIMENSIONS: 38" x 46"

MATERIALS: 42"-wide 100% cotton, color tested and preshrunk

Assorted prints (3 blue, 3 green, 3 yellow, 3 pink and 3 purple) for Butterfly blocks and borders: 1-3/4 yards total
Unbleached muslin for block backgrounds: 1-1/8 yards
Black solid for blocks: 1/4 yard
Backing: 1-1/2 yards
Binding: 1/2 yard blue plaid to make 178 inches of 1-1/2"-wide bias binding
Batting: 42" x 50"
Thread for piecing and quilting

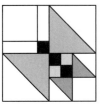 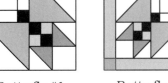

Butterfly #1
Make 10.

Butterfly #2
Make 10.

DIRECTIONS

BLOCKS:

Cutting amounts given are for each Butterfly #1 and #2 block. Amounts for whole quilt are in parentheses.

Butterfly #1: Make ten.

From assorted prints, cut:

2 (20) squares, 1-1/2" x 1-1/2" (Template #1)

1 (10) square(s), 3" x 3" (for half-square-triangle unit to be trimmed later to size of Template #2)

1 (10) square(s), 5" x 5" (for half-square-triangle unit to be trimmed later to size of Template #3)

From muslin, cut:

1 (10) square(s), 3" x 3" (for half-square-triangle unit to be trimmed later to size of Template #2)

1 (10) square(s), 5" x 5" (for half-square-triangle unit to be trimmed later to size of Template #3)

1 (10) square(s), 2-1/2" x 2-1/2" (Template #2)

1 (10) square(s), 3-1/2" x 3-1/2" (Template #4)

2 (20) rectangles, 1-1/2" x 3-1/2" (Template #5)

From black solid, cut:

3 (30) squares, 1-1/2" x 1-1/2" (Template #1)

Butterfly #2: Make ten.

From assorted prints, cut:

2 (20) squares, 1-1/4" x 1-1/4" (Template #6)

4 (40) squares, 1-1/2" x 1-1/2" (Template #1)

1 (10) square(s), 2-1/2" x 2-1/2" (for half-square-triangle unit to be trimmed later to size of Template #7)

1 (10) square(s), 4" x 4" (for half-square-triangle unit to be trimmed later to size of Template #4)

4 (40) rectangles 1-1/2" x 6-1/2" (Template #8)

From muslin, cut:

1 (10) square(s), 2-1/2" x 2-1/2" (for half-square-triangle unit, to be trimmed later to size of Template #7)

1 (10) square(s), 4" x 4" (for half-square-triangle unit to be trimmed later to size of Template #4)

1 (10) square(s), 2" x 2" (Template #7)

1 (10) square(s), 2-3/4" x 2-3/4" (Template #9)

2 (20) rectangles, 1-1/4" x 2-3/4" (Template #10)

From black solid, cut:

3 (30) squares, 1-1/4" x 1-1/4" (Template #6)

Piecing one Butterfly Block #1:

1. Place a 3" print square right sides facing with a 3" muslin square. Cut squares diagonally to make 2 triangle pairs. Using a 1/4" seam allowance, machine stitch the triangles together on the long side to make 2 squares. Press the seams toward the darker fabric. Measuring with a square cutting ruler, trim the resulting squares to 2-1/2" x 2-1/2" (Template #2).

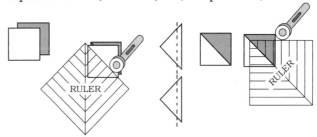

2. Repeat step 1 with the 5" squares to make the large two-triangle squares (Template #3). Trim to measure 4-1/2" including seam allowances.

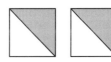

3. Make a fourpatch from print and black #1 squares.

4. Join the fourpatch, two #2 units and the muslin #2 square to make a 4-1/2" square.

5. Join the muslin 3-1/2" square (#4), two muslin rectangles (#5), and one black square #1 to make a 4-1/2" square unit.

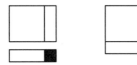

6. Join the 4 units as shown to complete the block.

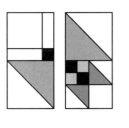 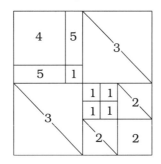

Piecing one Butterfly Block #2:

1. Using the same techniques and piecing order described for Butterfly Block #1, make a 6" Butterfly block. Use 2-1/2" x 2-1/2" print and muslin squares to make two-triangle square #7 (2" x 2"). Use 4" x 4" print and muslin squares to make two-triangle square #4 (3-1/2" x 3-1/2").

2. Join #8 print rectangles to top and bottom of pieced square. Join #1 print squares to either end of the remaining #8 rectangles and join units to sides of block as shown.

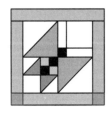 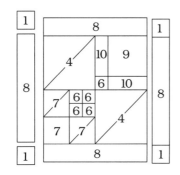

QUILT ASSEMBLY:

Arrange the finished blocks in rows, as shown in the Quilt Assembly Diagram on the facing page. Sew the rows together.

PIECED BORDER:

1. *From assorted prints, cut:*
   18 rectangles, 2-1/2" x 8-1/2" (no template)
   18 rectangles, 1-1/2" x 8-1/2" (no template)
   4 squares, 2" x 2" (Template #7)
   4 squares, 1-1/2" x 1-1/2" (Template #1)
   8 rectangles, 1-1/2" x 2-1/2" (Template #11)

2. Join 8-1/2"-long rectangles together in 18 pairs of one narrow and one wide as shown.

Make 18.

3. Make 4 corner squares as shown.

Make 4.

4. Join strip pairs together to form pieced border sections as shown in Quilt Assembly Diagram. Each side border contains 5 strip pairs and the top and bottom borders each contain 4 strip pairs. Join pieced border sections to sides of quilt first. Join pieced corner squares to top and bottom border sections and join to quilt.

FINISHING:

1. Plan and mark quilting design. Use outline quilting for most of the design. Gentle arcs in the Butterfly blocks imitate wing movement and antennae.

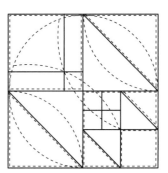

2. Layer batting, backing and quilt top. Baste.
3. Quilt by hand or machine.
4. Cut 178 inches of 1-1/2"-wide bias strips for binding.
5. Bind quilt edge.

Quilt Assembly Diagram

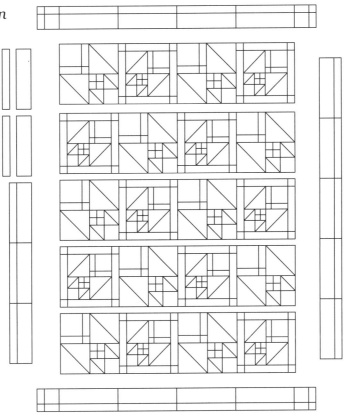

Templates

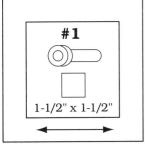

#1

1-1/2" x 1-1/2"

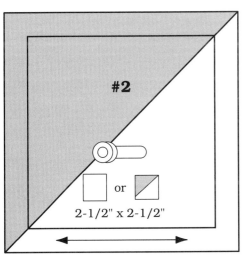

#2

or

2-1/2" x 2-1/2"

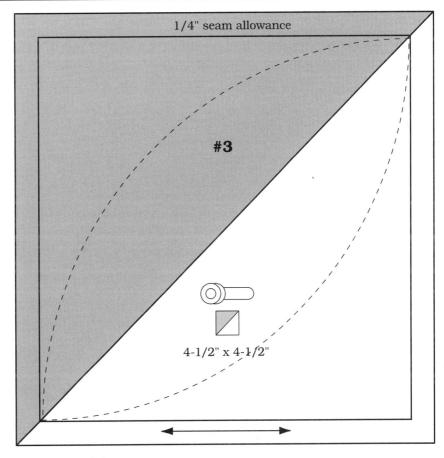

1/4" seam allowance

#3

4-1/2" x 4-1/2"

23

Templates (continued)

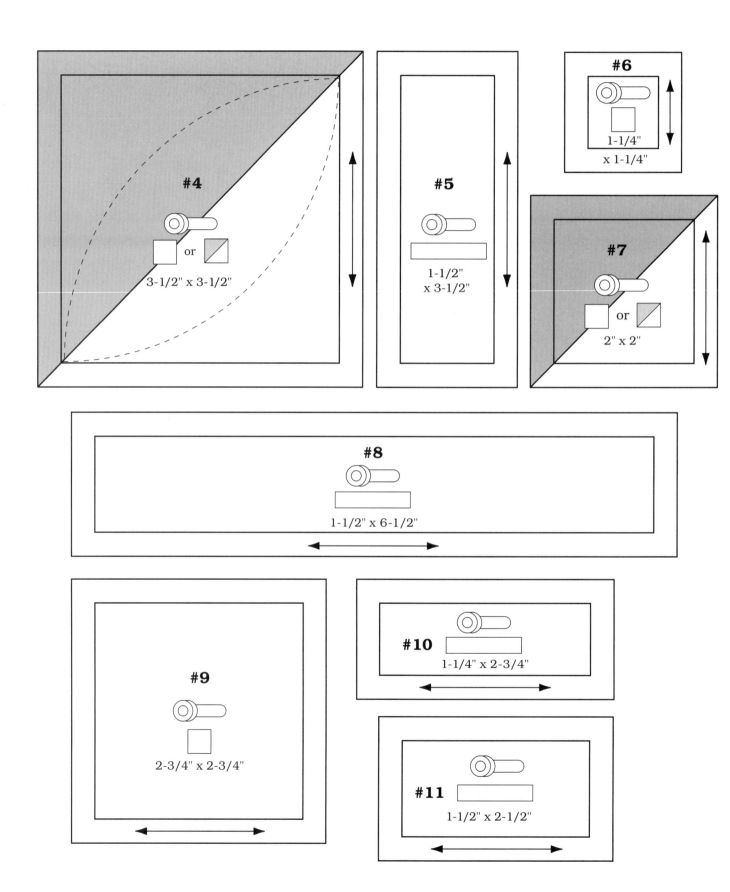

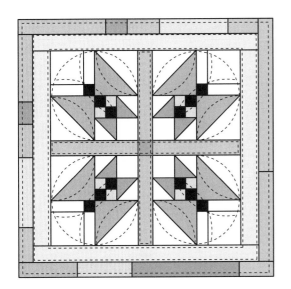

Butterfly Comfort Quilt

One grandma told me that as her grandchildren grew out of infancy, she would make them each a small portable version of their first baby quilts out of the scraps. The smaller "bankies" or comfort quilts were more portable and adaptable to various situations.

You'll probably have enough fabric left over from making Katie's Butterfly Quilt to make another little project. Use the 6" butterflies from the center of Block #2 to make a comfort quilt, wall hanging, doll quilt or pillow.

DIMENSIONS: 18" x 18"

MATERIALS: 42"-wide 100% cotton, color tested and preshrunk

Assorted prints, unbleached muslin, and black solid leftover from the Butterfly quilt on page 20.
Backing: 5/8 yard
Binding: leftovers to make 82 inches of 1-1/2"-wide bias binding
Batting: 20" x 20"
Thread for piecing and quilting

DIRECTIONS

BLOCKS: Make four 6" Butterfly blocks. See Cutting instructions for Butterfly #2 blocks on page 21. Omit #1 print squares and #8 print rectangles. See piecing instructions on page 22.

6" Butterfly Block
Make 4.

LATTICES AND CORNERSTONE: From assorted prints, cut 1 square 1-1/2" x 1-1/2" (#1 on page 23) and 4 rectangles 1-1/2" x 6-1/2" (#8 on page 24). Join cut pieces and pieced blocks in rows as shown in Quilt Assembly Diagram below. Join rows together.

INNER BORDER: Cut 2 strips 2" x 13-1/2" for sides and 2 strips 2" x 16-1/2" for top and bottom. Join to center section.

OUTER BORDER: Join random-length 1-1/2"-wide strips together end to end to make 2 strips 16-1/2" long and 2 strips 18-1/2" long. Join shorter strips to sides of center section first and longer strips last.

Quilt Assembly Diagram

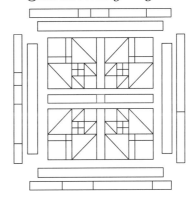

FINISHING:
1. Plan and mark quilting design.
2. Layer batting, backing and quilt top. Baste.
3. Quilt by hand or machine.
4. Cut 82 inches of 1-1/2"-wide bias strips for binding. Bind quilt edge.

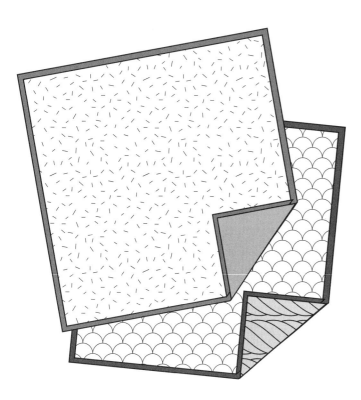

Receiving Blankets

At the suggestion of an experienced grandma, I made two of these warm and cozy receiving blankets for Katie Rose when she was born. I used fabrics to co-ordinate with her Butterfly quilt: flannel on one side, a storybook print on the other, and a plaid or striped print for the bias binding. Katie's mom raved about them so, I now make them for every newborn baby I know.

This project needs no quilting, just layer large fabric squares together and bind the edges. Be sure to preshrink your fabrics.

DIMENSIONS: 40" x 40"

MATERIALS: 42"-wide 100% cotton, color tested and preshrunk

Printed cotton: 1-1/4 yards
Printed cotton flannel: 1-1/4 yards
Plaid or stripe for binding: 1/2 yard
Thread

DIRECTIONS

1. Place printed cotton and cotton flannel pieces together with wrong sides together. Taking care to line up the selvages, press the two layers with an iron and pin to prevent shifting. Trim edges to make a double-layered 40" square.

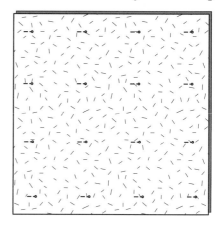

2. From the plaid or striped binding fabric, cut bias strips 1-1/2" wide. Join the ends of the strips as shown on page 11 to make a 170-inch length of bias binding, enough to go around the edges of the blanket with a few extra inches for joining.

3. Apply the binding around the outside edges of the 40" squares according to the Binding directions on page 11.

Katie Rose with her Great Grandfather Reynolds

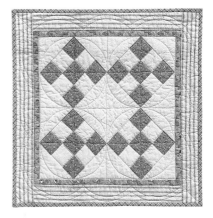

▲ **Ninepatch Doll Quilt** *by Marsha McCloskey, Seattle, WA, 1998, 17" x 17". Practice your machine quilting on this little quilt made from scraps from the Building Blocks Quilt.*

▲ **Building Blocks Quilt** *by Marsha McCloskey, Seattle, WA, 1998, 40" x 40". The center square of this quilt was left plain because the baby, the real star of the show, goes in the middle.*

Sailboat Wall Quilt ▶
by Marsha McCloskey, Seattle, WA, 1998, 15" x 13-1/2". For a quick shower gift, you can make this smaller version of the Sailboat Quilt in an afternoon.

Sailboat Quilt *by Marsha McCloskey,* ▶
Seattle, WA, 1998, 38" x 54". Quilted by Barbara Ford. Fitting a cars, trains and boats theme, this 1930s design is a great choice for a little boy.

◀ **Sunshine and Shadow Quilt**
*by Marsha McCloskey, Seattle,
WA, 1999, 40" x 40". Quilted by
Barbara Ford. A rainbow of
1930s reproduction prints make
this super-simple design a joyous
quilt to wrap around a baby.*

Katie's Butterfly Quilt *by
Marsha McCloskey, Seattle, WA,
1998, 38" x 46". The author
designed these pretty butterflies for
her son's first child, Katie Rose.*
▼

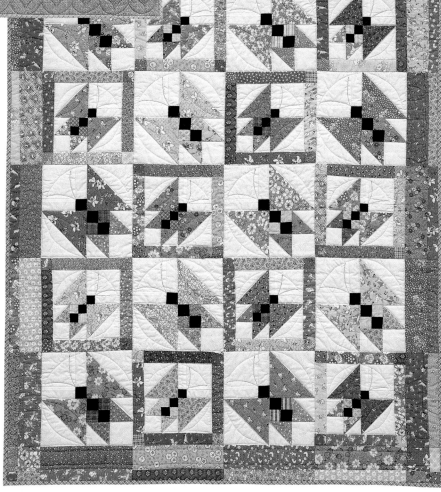

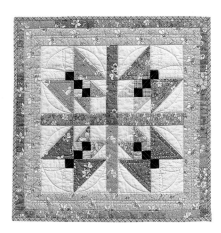

▲ **Butterfly Comfort Quilt** *by
Marsha McCloskey, Seattle, WA,
1998, 18" x 18". With leftover
fabric from Katie's Butterfly Quilt,
you can whip up this charming
little quilt to hang on the nursery
wall, wrap a favorite doll or
travel with baby in the car.*

Sara's Building Blocks Quilt ▶
*by Sara Nephew, Snohomish, WA,
1998, 35-1/2" x 40". Quilted by
Barbara Ford. For this design,
Sara has devised an ingenious
method for easy piecing without
set-in seams.*

◀ Stars and Pinwheels Quilt
*by Marsha McCloskey, Seattle,
WA, 1999, 38" x 38". Quilted by
Barbara Ford. Every baby's a
star wrapped in this pretty quilt.*

School House Quilt *by* ▶
Marsha McCloskey, Seattle,
WA, 1998, 39" x 51". Quilted
by Barbara Ford. House quilts
can be like a map for a child.
Which house belongs to Aunt
Jennifer? Where do Grandma
and Grandpa live?

◀ **Pinwheel Daisy Quilt** *by*
Marsha McCloskey, Seattle, WA,
1989, 41" x 52". Quilted by
Freda Smith. A traditional
design from the 1930s, these
charming pinwheels seem to
turn in the wind.

School House Quilt

House patterns are a traditional quilt favorite. This School House block is one I designed in the early 1980s.

In the quilt pictured on page 30, eighteen 6" School House blocks are set straight with 17 plain alternate blocks, surrounded by a wide plain inner border and scrappy, pieced sawtooth outer border. Choose 9 (make 2 houses of each print) or 18 (make one house of each print) different 1930s pastel reproduction prints for the houses and sawtooth border. Choose a muslin or plain-looking print for the background. My house blocks each contain only two fabrics, but you could make scrappy houses with many prints in each block.

DIMENSIONS: 39" x 51"

MATERIALS: 42"-wide 100% cotton, color tested and preshrunk

Assorted prints for the houses and sawtooth border: a fat quarter (18" x 22") of each of 9 different prints OR a fat eighth (9" x 22") of each of 18 different prints

Muslin or plain-looking print for block backgrounds, alternate blocks, inner border, and Sawtooth border: 2-1/2 yards

Backing: 1-3/4 yards

Binding: 5/8 yard blue plaid to make 190 inches of 1-1/2"-wide bias binding

Batting: 43" x 55"

Thread for piecing and quilting

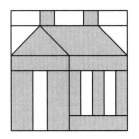

6" School House Block
Make 18.

DIRECTIONS

CUTTING: All cutting dimensions include 1/4"
seam allowance.

*From the 2-1/2-yard piece of background fabric,
make the following cuts, label the pieces and
set them aside for later:*

2 strips, each 3-1/2" wide, from lengthwise grain
for Inner Borders. Strips will be trimmed to
exact length later.

17 squares, each 6-1/2" x 6-1/2", for Alternate
Setting Squares

14 squares, each 7" x 7", for bias-strip pieced
Sawtooth Border

4 squares, each 2" x 2", for Sawtooth Border
corners

From the assorted prints, cut:

14 squares, each 7" x 7" for bias-strip pieced
Sawtooth Border

BLOCKS:

From the remaining background and print fabrics,
cut and piece 18 School House blocks.

*Numbers given are for one block with amounts for
the whole quilt in parentheses.*

From the assorted prints, cut:

3 (54) rectangles, 1-1/4" x 3-1/2" (Template #3)

3 (54) rectangles, 1-1/8" x 2-3/4" (Template #4)

2 (36) rectangles, 1-5/8" x 3-1/2" (Template #7)

2 (36) squares, 1-1/4" x 1-1/4" (Template #8)

1 (18) rectangle(s), 2" x 7-7/8" (Templates #5 & #6)

Cut #5 and #6 from one rectangle. Make 45°-angle
cuts from lower right and lower left corners as
shown. From lower left corner, measure and mark
4-1/4". Make 45°-angle cut from lower right to
upper left.

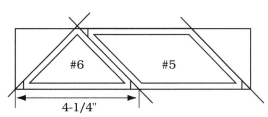

From the background fabric, cut:

3 (54) rectangles, 1-1/4" x 2" (Template #1)

1 (18) square(s), 2-3/8" x 2-3/8", cut diagonally to
yield 2 (36) half-square triangles (Template #2)

1 (18) rectangle(s), 1-1/4" x 3-1/2" (Template #3)

2 (36) rectangles, 1-1/8" x 2-3/4" (Template #4)

PIECING: Referring to the block diagram, arrange
pieces for one block. Join the patches in horizontal
rows as shown, then join rows together.

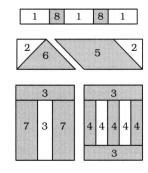

QUILT ASSEMBLY

Arrange the finished blocks in rows with the 6-1/2" alternate squares, as shown in the Quilt Assembly Diagram below. Sew the rows together.

Quilt Assembly Diagram

Inner Border

Note: *If you prefer not to do bias-strip piecing, use Template #2 on page 35 to cut 112 triangles from assorted prints and 112 triangles from the background fabric. Join print and background triangles to make two-triangle squares.*

2. Referring to the Quilt Assembly Diagram, join the two-triangle square units in borders rows. Make two side borders of 32 units each, and top and bottom borders of 24 units each. Notice that the direction of the diagonals changes in the middle of each border.

3. Join pieced side borders to the sides of the quilt. Add a 2" x 2" background square (Template #2) to each end of the top and bottom borders and join to the quilt.

FINISHING

1. Plan and mark quilting design. The long lines and houses can be quilted in the ditch. Make stiffened templates of the heart motif and the shaded half circle shape on page 34. Trace around the heart to make the four-heart quilting design for the plain alternate squares. Use the half circle to mark the Clamshell design in the Inner Border.
2. Layer batting, backing and quilt top. Baste.
3. Quilt by hand or machine.
4. Cut 190 inches of 1-1/2"-wide bias strips for binding. Bind quilt edge.

BORDERS

Inner Border: From the 3-1/2"-wide border strips, cut two strips 42-1/2" long for the side borders, and two strips 36-1/2" long for the top and bottom. (Measure your quilt before cutting! See Borders, page 8.) Join border strips to sides of quilt first, then to top and bottom.

Sawtooth Border:

1. Referring to the bias-strip piecing method outlined on page 7, use the fourteen 7" print squares and the fourteen 7" background fabric squares to make 112 two-triangle square units (Template #2) for the Sawtooth Border. Repeat steps 1 through 6 fourteen times.

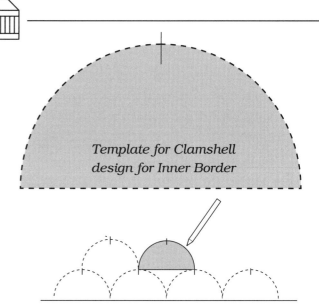

*Template for Clamshell
design for Inner Border*

Marking the Clamshell design

Note: *Photocopy the shaded templates
on this page. With a glue stick, glue each
shape face up on template plastic or
lightweight cardboard. With scissors,
carefully cut out shapes on the dashed line.
To mark quilting lines, place stiffened
templates face up on the right side of the
fabric. Hold firmly and with a removable
fabric marker, trace around each shape
onto the fabric.*

Quilting Motif for 6" Alternate Blocks

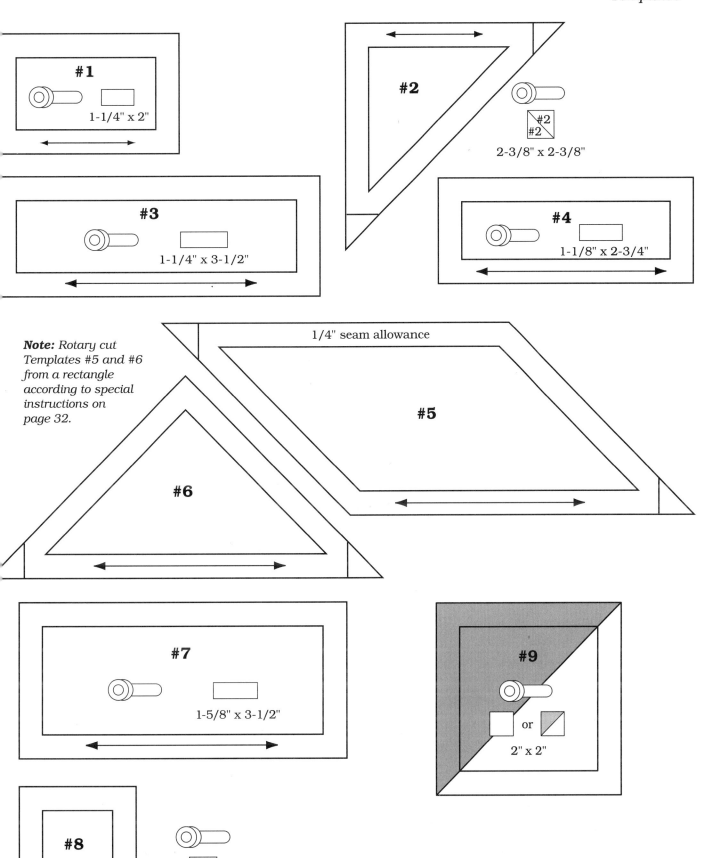

#1

1-1/4" x 2"

#2

#2
#2

2-3/8" x 2-3/8"

#3

1-1/4" x 3-1/2"

#4

1-1/8" x 2-3/4"

1/4" seam allowance

Note: *Rotary cut Templates #5 and #6 from a rectangle according to special instructions on page 32.*

#5

#6

#7

1-5/8" x 3-1/2"

#9

or

2" x 2"

#8

#8

1-1/4" x 1-1/4"

Pinwheel Daisy Quilt

The Pinwheel Daisy is a pattern from the 1930s that I first made for Sara Nephew's book, *My Mother's Quilts: Designs from the Thirties*. The quilt pictured on page 30 was made from authentic 1930s fabrics, the design has gentle machine-pieced curves and a hand-appliquéd circle in the center. The multi-colored borders around each block can be rotary cut, but the curved pieces are cut using traditional stiffened templates. The quilt really needs three kinds of colors: an assortment of brightly colored prints for the petals, a plain-looking light print or muslin for the background, and a bright accent fabric for the center circle.

DIMENSIONS: 41" x 52"

MATERIALS: 42"-wide 100% cotton, color tested and preshrunk

Assorted prints for daisy petals in blocks, lattice rectangles and squares: 1 yard total
Unbleached muslin for block backgrounds: 1 yard
Red polka dot for daisy centers: 1/8 yard
Pink print for borders: 1-1/2 yards
Backing: 1-5/8 yards
Binding, pink print: 5/8 yard to make 196 inches of 1-1/2"-wide bias binding
Batting: 45" x 56"
Thread for piecing and quilting

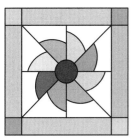

Pinwheel Daisy
11" block
Make 12.

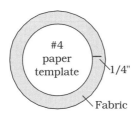

#4
paper
template

1/4"

Fabric

Cutting for
appliquéd
center circle.

DIRECTIONS

BLOCKS: Make 12 Pinwheel Daisy blocks.
*Cutting amounts are given for one Pinwheel Daisy block.
Amounts for whole quilt are in parentheses.*

From assorted prints, cut:
8 (96) of Template #1
4 (48) rectangles, 2" x 8-1/2" (Template #5)
4 (48) squares, 2" x 2" (Template #6)

From unbleached muslin, cut:
4 (48) of Template #2
4 (48) of Template #3

From red polka dot:
Make a 2" circle of paper (Template #4). Pin it
to the wrong side of red polka dot fabric and
add a 1/4" seam allowance as you cut around
it. Cut 1 (12).

Note: *To cut shapes from Templates #1, #2, and #3,
make* ***stiffened templates.*** *Photocopy the
templates on page 39. With a glue stick, glue each
shape face up on template plastic or lightweight
cardboard. With scissors, carefully cut out shapes
on the outside cutting line. Place stiffened templates
face up on the right side of the fabric. Hold firmly
and with a pencil or washable fabric marking pen,
trace around each shape onto the fabric. With sharp
fabric scissors, carefully cut out each fabric shape
just inside of the marked line.*

PIECING:

1. Make 4 Unit A. To sew the curved seam, place
   Template #2 on top of Template #1 with right
   sides facing. Match the starting edge for
   stitching with the trimmed points. With a 1/4"
   seam allowance, stitch slowly, pausing every
   4-5 stitches as you go. There is enough stretch
   in the top piece to accommodate the convex
   shape of the curve underneath. Press the seam
   allowance toward Template #1.

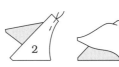

Unit A
Make 4.

2. Make 4 Unit B. Piece this unit the same way as
   Unit A, with Template #3 on top of Template #1.

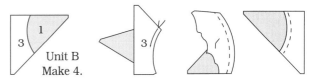

Unit B
Make 4.

3. Join the four A units to the four B units to
   make four square C units. Press seams toward
   A units.

Press.

B
A

Unit C

4. Matching diagonal opposing seams, sew the C
   units together to make two block halves.
   Matching at the center need not be terribly
   precise, as the center circle will be appliquéd
   over it. Press center seams to the left.

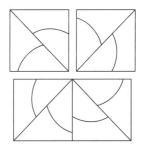

5. Match the centers of the block halves. Opposing
   vertical and diagonal seams will "nest." Pin, as
   shown on page 6 in the description of matching
   the center of a Pinwheel. Stitch center seam
   through the X. Press center seam to one side.

6. To prepare the red polka dot center circle for appliqué, turn the seam allowance over the paper's edge and baste the fabric to the paper. Ease fullness on the curve with a small running stitch. Press.

7. Leaving the paper in, appliqué the circle to the center of the pieced Pinwheel Daisy, using a blind stitch and the same color thread as the circle.

8. To remove the paper, turn the block to the wrong side and carefully cut away the pieced area behind the appliquéd circle, leaving 1/4" seam allowance. Remove the basting stitches and pull out the paper from the back.

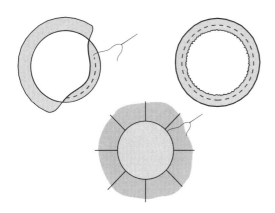

9. Add 2" x 8-1/2" border rectangles and 2" x 2" corner squares to blocks as shown.

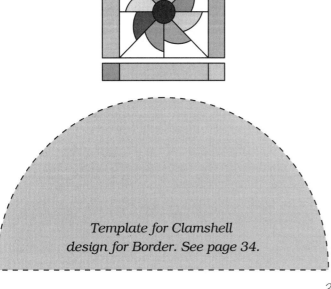

Template for Clamshell design for Border. See page 34.

QUILT ASSEMBLY: Arrange the finished blocks in rows, as shown in the Quilt Assembly Diagram. Sew the rows together in order to finish the center section of the quilt.

BORDER: From the pink border print, cut two strips 4-1/2" x 44-1/2" for the side borders and two strips 4-1/2" x 41-1/2" for the top and bottom. Join border strips to sides of quilt first, then to top and bottom.

Quilt Assembly Diagram

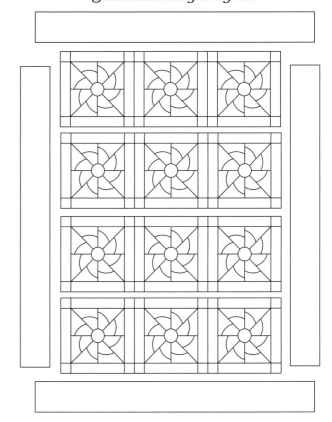

FINISHING:

1. Plan and mark quilting design. Outline quilt the blocks. Use the half-circle template to the left to mark the Clamshell design on the border (see page 34).

2. Layer batting, backing and quilt top. Baste.

3. Quilt by hand or machine.

4. Cut 196 inches of 1-1/2"-wide bias strips for binding. Bind quilt edge.

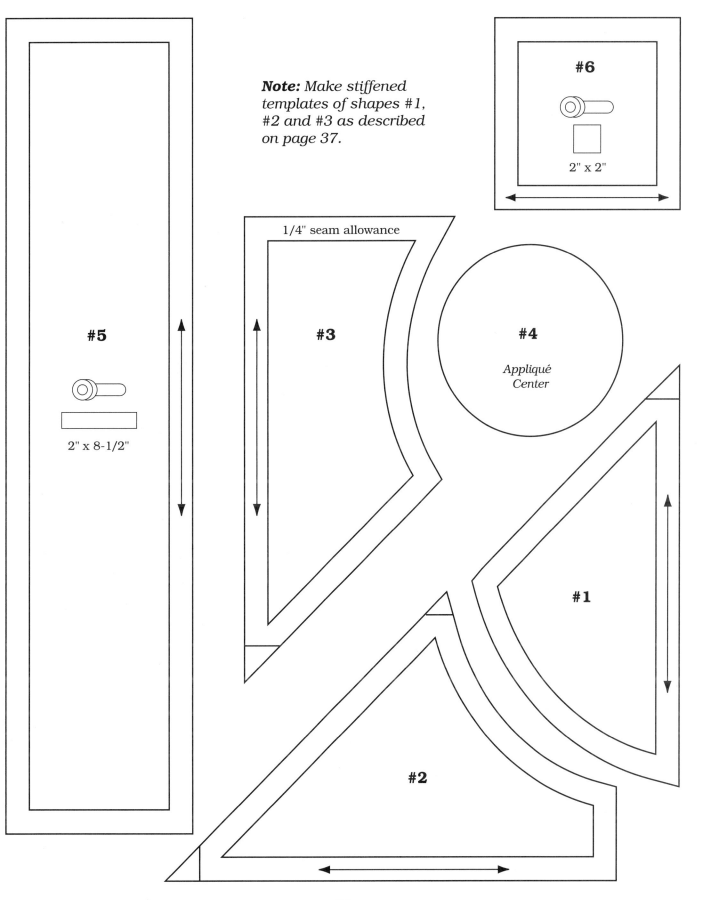

#6

2" x 2"

Note: *Make stiffened templates of shapes #1, #2 and #3 as described on page 37.*

#5

2" x 8-1/2"

1/4" seam allowance

#3

#4

Appliqué Center

#1

#2

Sailboat Quilt

My husband's best friend is a sailor. For a wedding gift, we gave him an Ocean Waves Quilt. His first child will get a sailboat quilt. This traditional pieced pattern is called the Mayflower. For the quilt pictured in color on page 27, I chose a red print with white stars and an unbleached muslin background, but scrappy 1930s reproduction prints would work just as well. Piecing the triangles is a breeze with the bias-strip piecing technique.

DIMENSIONS: 38" x 54"

MATERIALS: 42"-wide 100% cotton, color tested and preshrunk

Red print for Sailboat blocks: 1 yard
Unbleached muslin for block backgrounds and
    borders: 2-1/2 yards
Backing: 1-3/4 yards
Binding: 5/8 yard red and white stripe to make
    194 inches of 1-1/2"-wide bias binding
Batting: 44" x 58"
Thread for piecing and quilting

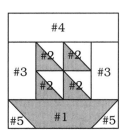

Sailboat
8" block
Make 24.

DIRECTIONS

BLOCKS: Make 24 Sailboat blocks.

Cutting amounts for one 8" Sailboat block are given first. Amounts for whole quilt are in parentheses.

From red print, cut:

stripe

1 (24) rectangle(s), 2-1/2" x 9-1/4" trim each end at 45° angle as shown (Template #1).

navy

4 squares, 13-1/2" x 13-1/2" for bias-strip pieced triangles for the whole quilt (Template #2)

From unbleached muslin, cut:

navy

2 (48) rectangles, 2-1/2" x 4-1/2" (Template #3)
1 (24) rectangle(s), 2-1/2" x 8-1/2" (Template #4)
1 (24) square(s), 2-7/8" x 2-7/8", cut diagonally to make 2 (48) half square triangles (Template #5)
4 squares, 13-1/2" x 13-1/2", for bias-strip pieced the triangles for the whole quilt (Template #2)

Piecing the Blocks:

Referring to the basic Bias-Strip Piecing Method on page 7, make 96 two-triangle square units, 4 for each Sailboat block.

Note: *If you prefer not to do bias-strip piecing, use Template #5 on page 43 to cut 96 triangles from the red print and 96 triangles from the background fabric. Join print and background triangles to make two-triangle squares.*

1. Place two 13-1/2" squares (1 red print and 1 unbleached muslin) right sides together. Cut strips 2-1/2" wide as pictured.

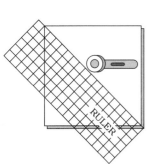 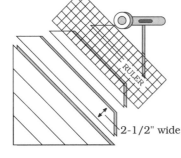

2-1/2" wide

2. Follow step 3 on page 7. Press seams toward print fabric. Sew bias strip pairs together as pictured and press.

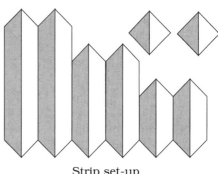

Strip set-up

3. Cut 30 two-triangle units, each 2-1/2" square from the set-up. (Cut squares slightly larger than 2-1/2", then trim to exact dimension. See page 7.)

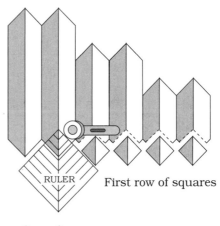

RULER   First row of squares

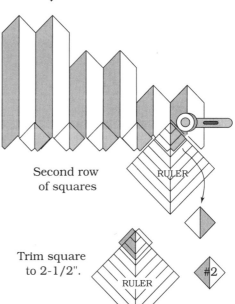

Second row of squares   RULER

Trim square to 2-1/2".   RULER   #2

4. Repeat Steps 1-3 three more times or until 96 units have been cut. There will be strips left over that can be used for the little Sailboat Wall Quilt on page 44.

Piecing the Sailboats:

1. Using 4 two-triangle units for each block, piece the "sail" of the boat as shown.

2. Make "hull" of the boat by adding a #5 unbleached muslin triangle to each end of the red #1 shape as shown.

3. Arrange pieced units with unbleached muslin #3 and #4 rectangles. Join pieces in rows as shown. Join rows together.

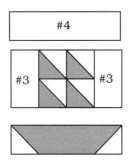

QUILT ASSEMBLY

Arrange the finished blocks in 6 rows of 4 blocks each, as shown in the Quilt Assembly Diagram. Sew the rows together.

BORDER

From unbleached muslin, cut two strips 3-1/4" x 48-1/2" for the side borders, and two, strips 3-1/4" x 38" for the top and bottom. (Measure your quilt before cutting! See Borders, page 8.) Join border strips to sides of quilt first, then to top and bottom.

FINISHING

1. Plan and mark quilting design. The quilt shown in color on page 27 was outline-quilted around the Sailboats. The red hull of the Sailboat (Template #1) contains a wave-like motif. The background of the blocks contains an allover fill of diagonal lines. The border was quilted using a commercial quilting stencil in a graceful chain design.
2. Layer batting, backing and quilt top. Baste.
3. Quilt by hand or machine.
4. Cut 194 inches of 1-1/2"-wide bias strips for binding. Bind quilt edge.

Quilt Assembly Diagram

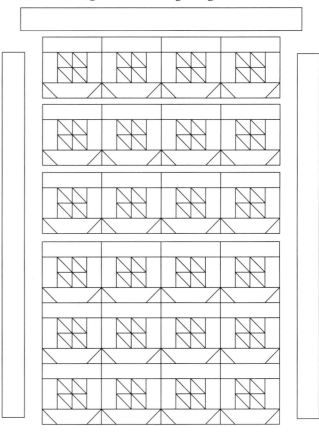

Templates
(8" block)

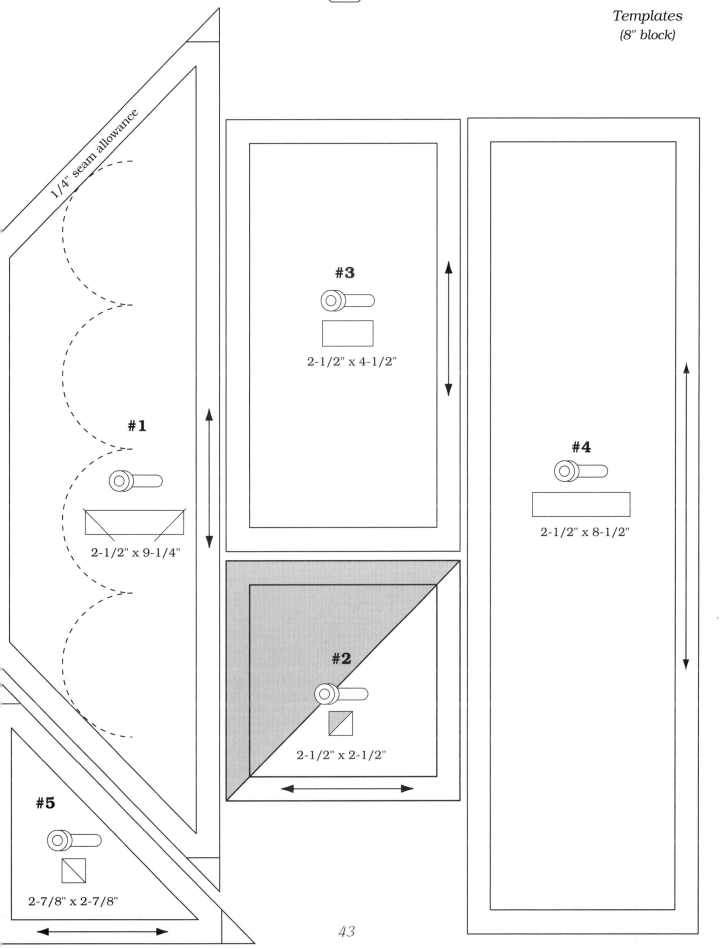

1/4" seam allowance

#1

2-1/2" x 9-1/4"

#3

2-1/2" x 4-1/2"

#2

2-1/2" x 2-1/2"

#4

2-1/2" x 8-1/2"

#5

2-7/8" x 2-7/8"

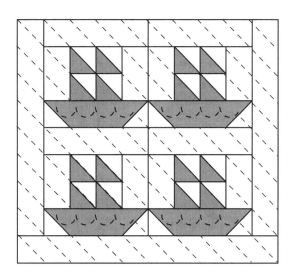

Sailboat Wall Quilt

From the fabric leftover from making the Sailboat Quilt on page 40, you can make this little wallhanging. I used four 6" Sailboat blocks in mine and machine quilted it with diagonal lines that follow the angles of the triangles.

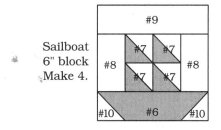

Sailboat 6" block Make 4.

DIMENSIONS: 15" x 13-1/2"

MATERIALS: 42"-wide 100% cotton, color tested and preshrunk

Red print for Sailboat blocks: fat quarter yard
Unbleached muslin for block backgrounds and borders: fat quarter yard
Backing: fat quarter yard
Binding, red and white stripe: fat quarter yard to make 67 inches of 1-1/2"-wide bias binding
Batting: 19" x 16"
Thread for piecing and quilting

DIRECTIONS

BLOCKS: Make 4 Sailboat blocks.
Cutting amounts for one 6" Sailboat block are given first. Amounts for whole quilt are in parentheses.

From red print, cut:
1 (4) rectangle(s), 2" x 7-1/4" (Template #6) trim each end at a 45° angle as shown.

2 squares, 7" x 7", for bias-strip pieced triangles for the whole quilt (Template #7)

From unbleached muslin, cut:
2 (8) rectangles, 2" x 3-1/2" (Template #8)
1 (4) rectangle(s), 2" x 6-1/2" (Template #9)
1 (4) square(s), 2-3/8" x 2-3/8", cut diagonally to make 2 (8) half-square triangles (Template #10)
2 squares, 7" x 7", for bias-strip pieced triangles for the whole quilt (Template #7)

Piecing the blocks:
Using leftover bias strips from the Sailboat quilt on page 40 or the bias-strip piecing method outlined on page 7, make 16 two-triangle square units, each 2" x 2" (4 for each sailboat block).

Referring to the piecing order for the 8" Sailboat block on page 42, piece four 6" Sailboat blocks.

QUILT ASSEMBLY
Arrange and sew the finished blocks in 2 rows of 2 blocks each, as shown in the Quilt Assembly Diagram. Sew the rows together.

BORDERS
From unbleached muslin, cut two strips 2" x 12-1/2" for the side borders, and one strip 2" x 15-1/2" for the bottom. (There is no top border strip.) Join border strips to sides of quilt first, then to bottom as shown.

FINISHING

1. Plan and mark quilting design.
2. Layer batting, backing and quilt top. Baste.
3. Quilt by hand or machine.
4. Cut 67 inches of 1-1/2"-wide bias strips for binding. Bind quilt edge.

Quilt Assembly Diagram

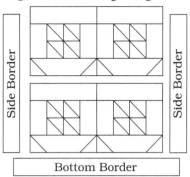

Sailboat Templates
(6" block)

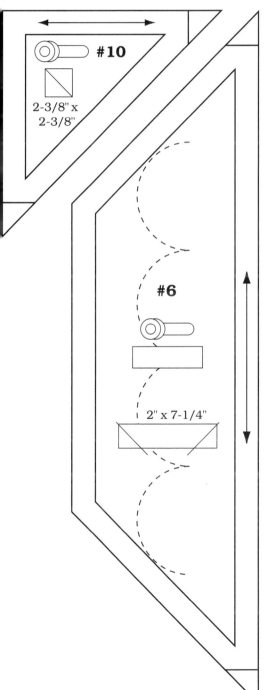

#10

2-3/8" x 2-3/8"

#6

2" x 7-1/4"

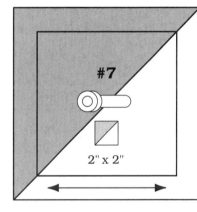

#7

2" x 2"

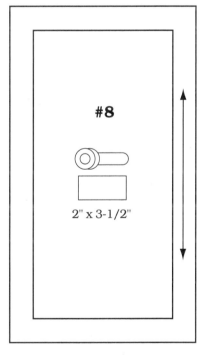

#8

2" x 3-1/2"

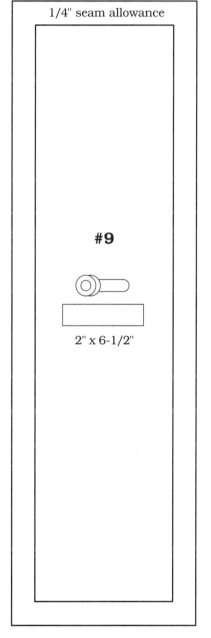

1/4" seam allowance

#9

2" x 6-1/2"

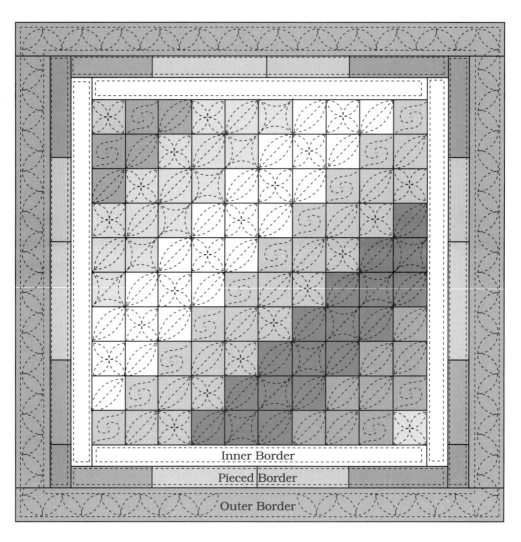

Inner Border

Pieced Border

Outer Border

Sunshine and Shadow Quilt

Five color groups are used in this easy-to-make little quilt pictured on page 28. I wanted a quilt that could be washed frequently and that would look great wrapped around a newborn. The 1930s pastel reproduction prints are soft and pretty. You'll need 3 different prints of each color. I used scraps from my fabric stash and bought a few fat quarters to round out the color selection. You'll need a 3-1/2" wide strip of each color ranging from 17-1/2" to 35" long, plus some leftovers for the pieced border (random-length rectangles cut 2" wide).

DIMENSIONS: 40" x 40"

MATERIALS: 42"-wide 100% cotton, color tested and preshrunk

3 blue prints: 1/8 yard each
3 pink prints: 1/8 yard each
3 yellow prints: 1/8 yard each
3 lavender prints: 1/8 yard each
3 green prints: 1/8 yard each
Light green plaid for inner border: 3/8 yard
Periwinkle print for outer border: 3/8 yard
Backing: 1-3/8 yards
Binding, yellow plaid: 1/2 yard to make 170 inches
    of 1-1/2"-wide bias binding
Batting: 44" x 44"
Thread for piecing and quilting

DIRECTIONS

All cutting dimensions include 1/4" seam allowance.

FABRIC SQUARES: Rotary cut a 3-1/2"-wide strip of each color and sub-cut the strip into the following 3-1/2" x 3-1/2" squares.

Blue #1:   5 squares
Blue #2:   5 squares
Blue #3:   5 squares
Pink #1:   5 squares
Pink #2:   5 squares
Pink #3:   6 squares
Yellow #1: 7 squares
Yellow #2: 8 squares
Yellow #3: 9 squares
Lavender #1: 10 squares
Lavender #2: 9 squares
Lavender #3: 8 squares
Green #1: 7 squares
Green #2: 6 squares
Green #3: 5 squares

Arrange the cut squares in diagonal color rows on a table or design wall. Play with the color order a bit until you are satisfied with the overall effect. Sew the squares together in color order to form 10 horizontal rows of 10 patches each. Join rows together.

INNER BORDER: From the light green plaid, cut two strips 2" x 30-1/2" for the side borders, and two strips 2" x 33-1/2" for the top and bottom. Join border strips to sides of quilt first, then to top and bottom.

PIECED BORDER: From leftover prints cut random length rectangles 2" wide. Sew them together end to end to make two strips 2" x 33-1/2" for the side borders, and two strips 2" x 36-1/2" for the top and bottom. Join border strips to sides of quilt first, then to top and bottom.

OUTER BORDER: From the periwinkle print, cut two strips 2-1/2" x 36-1/2" for the side borders, and and two strips 2-1/2" x 40-1/2" for the top and bottom. Join border strips to sides of quilt first, then to top and bottom.

FINISHING:
1. Plan and mark quilting design. The quilt pictured on page 28 was machine quilted with a different quilting motif in each diagonal color row.
2. Layer batting, backing and quilt top. Baste.
3. Quilt by hand or machine.
4. Cut 170 inches of 1-1/2"-wide bias strips for binding. Bind quilt edge.

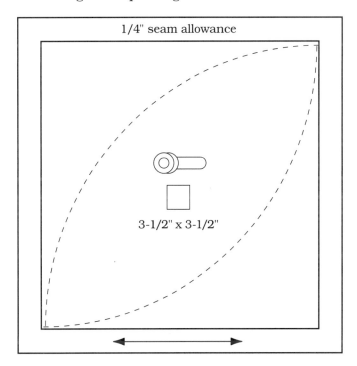

1/4" seam allowance

3-1/2" x 3-1/2"

Sara's Baby Blocks Quilt

DIMENSIONS: 35-1/2" x 40"

Sara Nephew is a quilt designer and a grandma to two adorable little girls. Her quilting specialties are designs made from 60°-angle patches, and fabric and color combinations from the 1930s. Sara designed and made this traditional Baby Blocks quilt. You'll notice, though, that her cutting and construction techniques are right up-to-date. There are no set-in seams in Sara's method of construction. If you use her special ruler, the Super 60 (ordering information is on page 50), rotary cutting the patches is a breeze. If you don't have the Super 60, use conventional cutting rulers or templates to cut the patches.

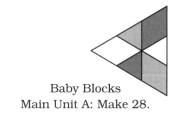

Baby Blocks
Main Unit A: Make 28.

Left Fill-in
Unit B: Make 4.

Right Fill-in
Unit C: Make 4.

MATERIALS: 42"-wide 100% cotton, color tested and preshrunk

Assorted rainbow dark prints: 3/4 yard total
Assorted rainbow medium prints: 3/4 yard total
Assorted rainbow light prints: 3/4 yard total
   (You'll need at least a 6" width of each fabric to allow for shrinkage, off-grain weaves, etc.)
Yellow print for borders and binding (1/2 yard to make 172 inches of 1-1/2-wide bias binding): 1-1/4 yards total
Backing: 1-1/4 yards
Batting: 40" x 44"
Thread for piecing and quilting

DIRECTIONS

COLOR PLANNING: With colored pencils, color the quilt *Color Chart* below in diagonal rows of diamonds. Use the color photo on page 29 and the shaded drawing on the facing page as guides. Each color group needs a dark, a medium and a light fabric (for instance, a dark blue, a medium blue and light blue) to make the Baby Blocks look three dimensional. Make this color chart correspond with the fabrics you have chosen and refer to it while cutting the diamonds and triangles.

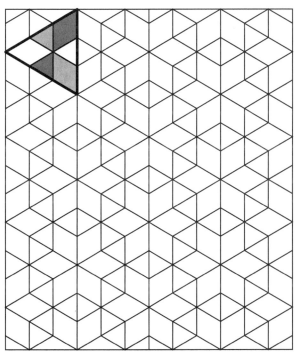

Color Chart

CUTTING AND PIECING: Cut diamonds and triangles to make 28 of Main Unit A. Assemble as pictured below. Each Unit A contains:
   1 dark diamond (Template #1)
   1 medium diamond (Template #1)
   1 light diamond (Template #1)
   1 dark triangle (Template #2)
   1 medium triangle (Template #2)
   1 light triangle (Template #2)

Cut diamonds and triangles to make 4 of Left Fill-in Unit B. Assemble as pictured below. Each Unit B contains:
   1 dark diamond (Template #1)
   1 medium triangle (Template #2)
   1 light triangle (Template #3)
   1 light triangle (Template #4)

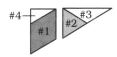

Cut diamonds and triangles to make 4 of Right Fill-in Unit C. Assemble as pictured below. Each Unit C contains:
   1 medium diamond (Template #1)
   1 dark triangle (Template #2)
   1 light triangle (Template #3)
   1 light triangle (Template #4 reversed)

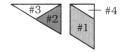

QUILT ASSEMBLY:

Arrange the finished units in rows, as shown in the Quilt Assembly Diagram. Sew the rows together.

BORDER

From the yellow border print, cut two strips 5-1/2" x 30-1/2" for the side borders and two strips 5-1/2" x 35-1/2" for the top and bottom. (Measure the quilt center before cutting.) Join border strips to sides of quilt first, then to top and bottom.

FINISHING

1. Plan and mark quilting design. Use outline quilting on the piecing. The quilting design drawn in the border (on page 48) was made using the finished size of the #2 template (on page 51) to create a design.
2. Layer batting, backing and quilt top. Baste.
3. Quilt by hand or machine.
4. Cut 172 inches of 1-1/2"-wide bias strips for binding. Bind quilt edge.

Quilt Assembly Diagram

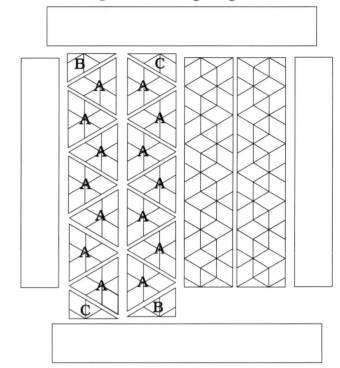

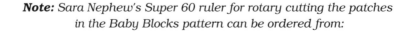

Note: *Sara Nephew's Super 60 ruler for rotary cutting the patches in the Baby Blocks pattern can be ordered from:*

Clearview Triangle
8311 180th St. S.E.
Snohomish, WA 98296-4802
Call toll-free: 1-888-901-4151

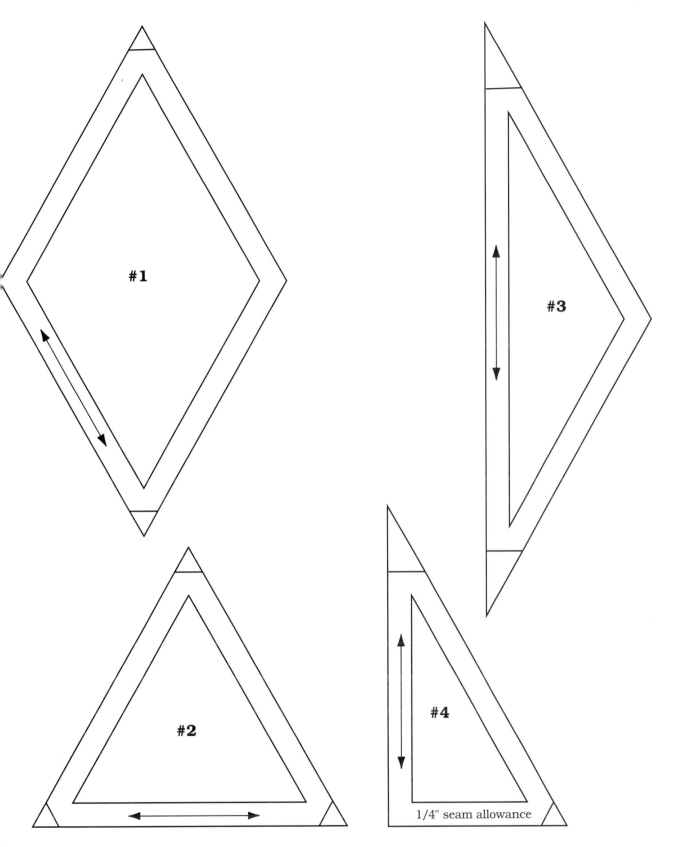

#1

#2

#3

#4

1/4" seam allowance

Squishy Patchwork Block

When my own children were little, I sold patchwork gift items at craft fairs. One toy I made was a fabric cube with a different appliquéd design on each of the six sides. I made the patchwork block shown here (a color photo is on the back cover) for Katie Rose out of scraps from her quilt. Stitching so the seam allowances along the edges of the cube were on the outside gave it a fuzzy, chenille-like appearance. At an early age, her tiny fingers could grasp the block by the seam allowances.

DIMENSIONS: 5" x 5" x 5"

MATERIALS: 42"-wide 100% cotton, color tested and preshrunk

> Print fabric scraps from other projects
> White fabric for lining: 1/4 yard
> Polyester Stuffing
> Thread for piecing

DIRECTIONS

1. Make six 3" patchwork blocks using scraps from other projects. I used leftover bias strips from the School House quilt on page 31 to cut 1-1/2" two-triangle squares (Template #1). I then added 1-1/2" unpieced squares (Template #1) of various prints and backgrounds to make the simple ninepatch-based designs pictured here. Each block should measure 3-1/2" x 3-1/2" including seam allowances.

2. Use Templates #2, #3 and #4 to cut rectangles from various prints. Join to pieced blocks to make borders as shown on the facing page.

3. Cut 6 white and 6 print squares, 5-1/2" x 5-1/2". Layer each pieced block with a white square, then a print one. Pin or machine quilt layers together. Make six 3-layered squares.

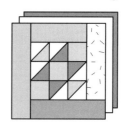

4. Treating each 3-layered square as one piece, stitch the squares together to make a cube. Place squares wrong sides facing. Use a 1/2" seam allowance: raw edges will be on the outside of the cube. Begin and end stitching 1/2" from the raw edge; backtack at the start and finish.

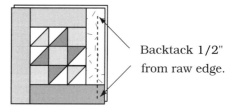

Backtack 1/2" from raw edge.

5. Join four layered squares in a row, then add the top and bottom squares to make a cube (follow the numbered sequence). Leave one side open for stuffing.

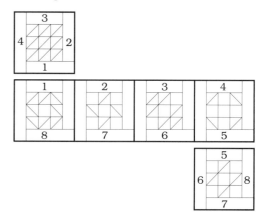

6. Stuff the cube loosely with polyester stuffing. Stitch last side seam closed. Trim raw seam allowance edges to 3/8" or 1/4". Wash by hand and dry in the dryer to make the edges fuzzy.

Assembly Diagrams

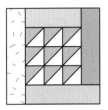 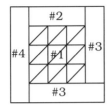

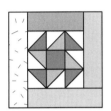 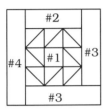

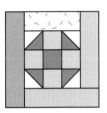 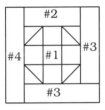

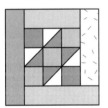 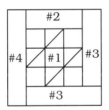

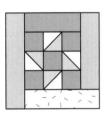 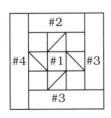

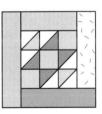 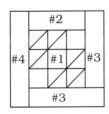

Templates

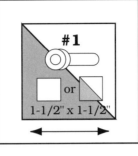

#1
or
1-1/2" x 1-1/2"

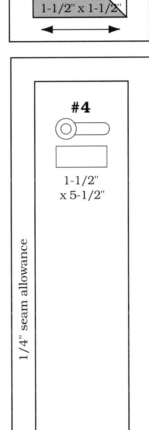

1/4" seam allowance

#4
1-1/2"
x 5-1/2"

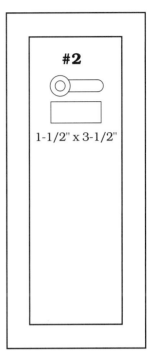

#2
1-1/2" x 3-1/2"

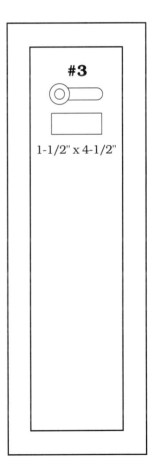

#3
1-1/2" x 4-1/2"

#5

#5
#5
1-7/8" x 1-7/8"

Note: *If you prefer not to do bias-strip piecing, use Template #5 to cut triangles to make the two-triangle square units in these block designs.*

Patchwork Baby Ball

My sister made a soft ball of pentagonal patches for my kids when they were little. My son and his daddy would throw it around the house for hours. It was easy for little fingers to grasp and it wouldn't hurt furniture or bounce very far. Over the years I made lots of these balls (the geometric name for them is dodecahedron!) as gifts: I chose brightly colored patches and cross-stitched the seams with embroidery floss.

This ball (pictured in color on the back cover) is made with 1930s pastel prints and is pieced with the seam allowances on the outside to update the style and cut down on handwork.

DIMENSIONS: approx. 15" in circumference

MATERIALS: 42"-wide 100% cotton, color tested and preshrunk

12 assorted prints: a 4" x 4" scrap of each
Polyester stuffing
Thread for piecing

DIRECTIONS

1. Using the template on page 55, cut 12 pentagons, each of a different fabric.

2. Divide the pentagon patches into two groups of six. With wrong sides together so the seams will be on the outside, stitch 5 patches together as pictured. Begin and end each line of stitching with a little backtack. Sew from seam line to seam line stopping 1/4" from the edge of the fabric.

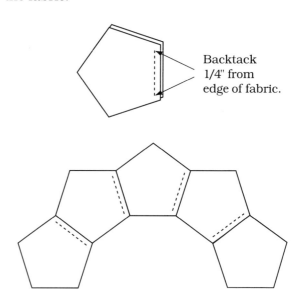

Backtack
1/4" from
edge of fabric.

3. With the seam allowances on the outside, join the sixth patch to the other five to make half of the ball. Follow the order given and sew six seams. Repeat for the other half of the ball.

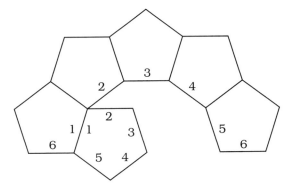

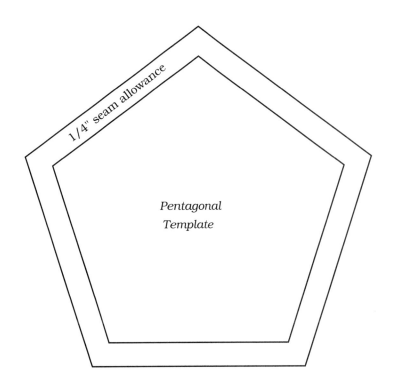

1/4" seam allowance

Pentagonal Template

4. Join the two halves in the same manner until only three seams are left open.

5. With polyester stuffing, stuff the ball to the desired firmness with. Overstuffing the ball will make it harder to stitch the final three seams, so keep it squishy.

6. Stitch the last three seams closed. I basted mine closed by hand before machine stitching.

TOOLS AND SUPPLIES

Sewing Machine: It needn't be fancy. All you need for piecing is an evenly locking straight stitch. Get to know your sewing machine. Have it serviced if necessary, so it is in good working order.

Even-feed or Walking Foot: This sewing machine attachment is for sewing through multiple thicknesses and feeding them evenly. Use it for bindings and for machine quilting.

Iron and Ironing Board: A shot of steam is useful.

Pins: Multi-colored glass-headed pins are easy to find when dropped on the rug. A magnetic pin holder keeps them from spilling.

Needles: Sewing machine needles need to be changed often. Keep a supply of new needles for light- to medium-weight fabrics on hand. You'll also need an assortment of hand-sewing needles, known as "sharps," and quilting needles, called "betweens" (size #8, #9 or #10).

Scissors: A pair for cutting paper, a pair for cutting fabric and one for snipping threads.

Seam Ripper: Keep one handy, just in case.

Fabric Markers: You will need a pen or pencil for marking quilting lines; check at your fabric store for different marking tools. Whatever marking product you choose, test it first on scraps of the fabrics used in your quilt to make sure the marks are removable.

Permanent marking pens are available in many colors. Use them for messages you want written on your quilt (front or back) and to properly sign your quilt with your name, date and location the quilt was made.

Sewing Thread: For machine piecing, use 100% cotton, neutral-colored thread, as light as the lightest fabric in your quilt. Choose one color of thread and use it throughout the quilt. Use a dark neutral thread for piecing dark solids. For stitching down bindings, you will need thread to match the binding fabric.

Quilting Thread: Special hand quilting thread is available at your local quilt shop in a variety of colors. It is slightly heavier than sewing thread and is specially coated to help prevent snarling. For hand quilting, I generally pick one color and use it for the whole quilt, but there's no rule to prevent you from matching threads to fabrics.

For machine quilting, I use DMC 50 Embroidery cotton thread in colors that blend with the surface colors of the quilt. This might mean using several thread colors on the same quilt, *i.e.*, white on white, navy on navy, red on red.

Rotary Cutter: These come in different sizes and styles. I usually use one with a 2"-diameter blade. Choose a style that fits comfortably in your hand and keep a fresh refill blade handy. The blades are very sharp, but become dull with use and are easily nicked.

Rotary Cutting Mat: Made of various plastic materials, these mats come in several sizes and are necessary in order to use your rotary cutter. Most brands are neutral green in color and have some sort of gridded markings. Choose a harder "self-healing" surface over a soft one that may wear out quickly with only normal use. My favorite mat measures 24" x 36" and covers half of my work table. I have a smaller mat to carry with me when I sew away from home.

Removable Tape: Use removable tape for taping paper templates to cutting rulers and for holding tracing paper in place.

Cutting Rulers: Rulers for rotary cutting are 1/8"-thick transparent Plexiglass™ and come in a variety of sizes and markings. The key elements in selecting rotary cutting rulers are that they be accurate and have suitable markings for the job at hand. I look for multi-purpose rulers rather than task-specific or template-like shapes. It's a good idea to use rulers from the same manufacturer because the markings are more likely to be consistent from one ruler to the next.

Though I own many rotary cutting rulers, these are the ones I use the most:
1. A 6" x 24" ruler for cutting long strips. It is marked in 1", 1/4" and 1/8" increments (that's important!) with both 45°- and 60°-angle guidelines.
2. A 15" square marked in 1", 1/4" and 1/8" increments for cutting large squares.
3. A 3" x 18" or 6" x 12" ruler for shorter cuts and medium-sized pieces, where the previous two rulers are too large.
4. An 8" square ruler marked in 1/8" increments with a 45°-angle line running corner to corner is extremely handy for cutting two-triangle squares and a variety of other functions.